MAKING MARRIAGE WORK

Making MARRIAGE Work

Truman Esau, M.D.
with Beverly Burch

VICTOR BOOKS®
A DIVISION OF SCRIPTURE PRESS PUBLICATIONS INC.
USA CANADA ENGLAND

© 1990 by SP Publications, Inc.

Portions of this book were originally printed by Victor Books in 1986 under the title *Partners in Process.*

Scripture quotations are from the *Holy Bible, New International Version,* © 1973, 1978, 1984, International Bible Society. Used by permission of Zondervan Bible Publishers.

Library of Congress Cataloging-in-Publication Data

Esau, Truman G.
  Making marriage work / by Truman G. Esau with Beverly J. Burch.
    p. cm.
  Includes bibliographical references.
  ISBN 0-89693-727-5
  1. Marriage—Religious aspects—Christianity. I. Burch, Beverly.
II. Title
BV835.E815 1990
248.8'44—dc20   89-60165
                                                                   CIP

c o n t e n t s

To Marilyn

whose depth of fellowship with Christ
has sustained me these many years

preface

On a recent vacation, my wife, Marilyn, and I spent a long day driving through Central Vermont. Her forebears had settled there after battling in the American Revolution, and we often enjoy hunting for the gravesites of her maternal ancestors when we are in that area. On this trip we planned to visit the grave of a recently deceased uncle, and we also wanted to find the Baptist church her great-great-uncle had served as its first pastor.

I was sure the gravesite was near her mother's family's plot in the old Middletown graveyard. I could picture clearly, from our last visit, the exact spot, with wild raspberries draped over the stone. My memory was so vivid, I was certain it was accurate. However, Marilyn was equally certain that the gravesite was in a different cemetery, and she described in detail how to get there.

As the discussion continued, we discovered that we also had conflicting impressions of where the church was. Although we both remembered it as being in Middletown, we had different mental images of the exact spot.

The intensity of our discussion led us to abandon, for the moment, the logistics of our travel, and to talk about the meanings and feelings lying beneath the surface of our interaction (a conversational luxury our busy day-to-day life seldom affords us—to our loss).

What came out were some of the issues of power that so permeate our society today, and we had nineteen years of marriage from which to draw examples to illustrate our points. By temperament, I am the more likely to dominate, but Marilyn, being human, has her moments too. How painful to discover the ways we may have run roughshod over each other's feelings and damaged the trust we value so highly between us. But that very pain, and the love we hold for each other, kept us talking, working to sort out what was going on between us.

Long past are the days when we might need reassurance of each other's love, but every marriage needs the nurturing, renewal, and reinforcement of honest communication. Though temporarily painful, our conversation rewarded us with a richer understanding of each other and a deeper sense of connectedness and trust. At the same time, our fellowship with Christ was renewed, for He was very much a part of our talk as we yearned for unbroken awareness of His favor.

Quite a journey, that conversation in the car. It brought us fully up to date with each other, refreshed us in many ways. We had had no conscious awareness, at the outset, that we had needed such a talk, but something deep inside must have told us that we did.

That's the way it is with any vital relationship, and that's what this book is about—the process of back-and-forth interchange between husband and wife that lends life and growth to a marriage. In spite of all the mixed reviews marriage has received in recent decades, we are still people in need of relationship, longing for someone to whom to bond and belong. There is no better arena than marriage for that kind of intimacy. It is a relationship designed to reflect no less than the strong love Christ has for His bride, the church. Marriage is indeed sanctified ground.

As it turned out, Marilyn was right about where the cemetery was; I had confused her uncle's grave with her grandfather's. And I was right about the location of the church; Marilyn had confused the area with a neighboring community. That pretty much confirmed the conclusion our discussion had already led us to—that we are equal and of equal value before Jesus Christ.

Truman Esau, M.D.
Truro, Massachusetts
1990

part 1

THE MAKING OF A MARRIAGE

o n e

The Triumph of Marriage

T he husband and wife who sat before me both felt anxious, bewildered, and defeated. However, they communicated those feelings in different ways. She wore the gray, beaten-down expression of someone who doesn't want to try anymore—which, in fact, was the case. It was her suicidal despair that had brought them to my office.

His clipped, assertive description of their situation barely covered an irritation energized by the terror he felt as he watched their carefully constructed world crumble around them.

As I listened to their story, my conviction grew that Pete and Jean were not bad people. Nor were they strikingly unusual. But there was no question that they and their marriage were in trouble.

Pete and Jean had met on a classic, storybook spring day when both were juniors at a Christian college. Both were committed Christians actively seeking God's will for their lives and willing to do whatever that entailed. It was that shared commitment that drew them together at first, but it was the discovery of how much they enjoyed each other, how at home they felt in each other's company, that led them to spend more and more time together.

When the idea of marriage first began to dawn on them, it seemed to be too delightful to be true. Surely God must want them to be willing to give each other up in favor of following Him. But self-probing, questioning, and hours of prayer only deepened their conviction that they should be together. So the week after graduation, they were married with the blessing of family, friends, and the Lord.

Their first years of marriage were a delight of warmth, togetherness, and discovery. By day they talked constantly, sharing their thoughts and feelings, and found more and more that they held in common, until they grew to feel as if they could almost read each other's minds. By night, bursts of sexual passion and the warm comfort of snuggling into each other's arms wrapped them in security and contentment. Their commitment to each other, already firm on their wedding day, deepened.

Confident in each other and in their marriage, they launched into parenthood, unaware that their tiny son would bring with him the first warning tremors of the quake that would later shake the very foundations of their marriage. It wasn't just the tiredness, the stress of adjustment, the topsy-turvy schedule, the daily uncertainty of deciphering little Ben's cries and needs that caused the rumblings. It was a deeper, unacknowledged panic that began to grip Pete at the core of his being.

In those early months of parenthood, Pete's fears were virtually imperceptible. What showed was a tightening of his grip on life and on their household. As the years went by and two more children came, he clenched his jaw a little tighter, worked harder and longer hours at his job, and became more and more moralistic in his administration of his family.

Gone were the days of free and happy chatter with Jean. Gone were the cozy, intimate nights. Daytime conversations became business meetings to keep the household running, and nighttime intimacy was laden with tension.

Ironically, it was Pete's desire to be a good father that fueled the couple's problems. He had vivid memories of the pain his own father had caused as he was growing up. Bombastic and intimidating, Pete's father had demanded unquestioning obedience from his wife and sons while at the same time reserving the right to do what he pleased with his own life. What he pleased included nightly visits at the local tavern and weekend flings with the women he met there.

Squandering the better part of his biweekly paychecks on those nights out, he left his wife to manage the household as well as she could on what was left. Because their mother had to scrimp to get by, the boys went without many of the things they would have liked to have, and during their school years they often endured classmates' snickers and snide remarks at their patched jeans and re-sale bicycles. By the time they were teenagers, they were adept at fabricating cover stories to explain why they never attended any of the school's social functions or invited friends to their house.

Pete's resentment flared every time he remembered his father's capricious and cruel dictatorship. When, as a teen-ager, he had become a Christian, he had vowed to himself that if he ever had a family, he would not repeat his father's mistakes.

When his own children were born, his secret fear that he might, after all, turn out like his father, drove him to work hard at undoing his childhood experience. Without consulting Jean (in fact, without being aware that he ought to consult her), he began constructing his own standards of what a father ought to be. High on his list was a rigid morality that often verged on legalism, which he exacted of his family as well as of himself. At the same time, he labored to make sure his children had every material benefit that they could possibly want. They were not going to suffer the humiliating deprivations he had suffered!

Because the changes in Pete had started so gradually, Jean at first was not disturbed. She was proud of Pete's dedication to being a good father, and his hard work gave her a sense of security and confidence.

But as the children grew, she became uncomfortable with what she saw as unreasonable expectations of their behavior and the harshness of the punishments meted out for ordinary childish pranks. Not an outspoken or self-confident woman, her protests at first were mild, tentative questions. But Pete, perceiving her questions as efforts to undermine his authority, had cut them off sharply, tightened his grip, and become remote and critical.

Fearful of losing Pete's love, Jean swallowed her questions. Her own father had been quite strict, and as a child she had learned compliance as a way of gaining his love. In the face of Pete's anger she reverted to her childhood tactic. But the more she complied, the more distant she felt from Pete. As the years went by, her frustration mounted.

When the children became teenagers and Pete seemed even more rigorous in his attempts to control their behavior, Jean once again found it in herself to speak up. She remembered how painful her own adolescence had been under a demanding father, and she didn't want her children going through the same experience.

Arguments erupted, driving the couple further and further apart. For a short while the house was a battleground, but in the end, Jean again backed down. The years of marriage had taken their toll on what little self-confidence she had possessed, and Pete seemed so sure of himself, and so well-supported by the Scriptures he quoted. Intimidated and discouraged, Jean withdrew into herself. Despairing of an outlet, her fears and resentment and loneliness lodged deep within her and sapped her spirit.

So there Pete and Jean were—stuck. Repeated attempts to resolve their conflicts seemed only to tighten the tangle and intensify the pain. Yet because of personal convictions about the permanence of their marriage vows, neither of them even considered the idea of divorce. Their sense of obligation to their marriage commitment held them together but also heightened their resentment of each other.

Caught in their parents' marital standoff, their children found themselves in no-man's-land. They chafed under Pete's strictness but had no answer to the Scripture passages he quoted. And they saw him as the key to having designer clothes and a car upon high school graduation. They sympathized with Jean's pain but were frustrated and embarrassed by her inability to stand up for herself or for them. They had no idea who was right or wrong and ended up carrying a vague sense of guilt for causing their parents' problems.

What had once appeared to be a close family became a house full of silent, remote, lonely strangers.

It took many weeks to unravel the tangled snarl that the family had become, and to trace the threads to their sources in Pete's and Jean's original families and the early intertwining of their relationship. And of course, the unsnarling sometimes involved some painful yanking at the threads before they loosened to reveal the intricacy of the knots.

But in spite of the discomfort, they kept at it. Pete and Jean were essentially strong and honest people, and they were eventually rewarded for their perseverance. They began to find new joy and freedom in their relationship, which in turn began to free their children.

What had gone wrong? How had two upright, responsible, and sincere Christians ended up in such a marital tangle?

As we worked things through, it became evident that although their relationship had been founded on a fiercely held commitment to God and to marital fidelity, they had stopped short of allowing themselves to become deeply bonded to one another. Though unshakably committed to each other, the two had never really become one. They had never gotten to the point where each thoroughly trusted the other's love and acceptance. They had always kept the core of their being—the place where they felt vulnerable and fallible and, yes, sinful—carefully protected from each other. Their inner lives had been so sealed off, like the scene of a crime, that they were profoundly fearful of discovery. Each held the secret belief that if they were really known, they would be rejected, and that their spouse's love would turn back at the sight of anything that was not good.

Early in their relationship, they had been on the way to developing a loving bond. Their days had been rich in the kind of freedom and sharing that draw two lives into one. But latent fears, activated by parenthood, had taken hold and choked the growth of their intimacy. Unaware of this, they had allowed each other to slip from the number-one place in their hearts. Their children, rather than each other, had become their primary focus. But parenthood, unless fed by a strong marriage, can be draining, and both Pete and Jean had ended up feeling unnurtured, resentful, and alone.

Now, as they persisted in prayer and therapy, their original enjoyment and valuing of each other began to creep back into their relationship, and a new dimension was added as well. Able for the first time in their relationship to hear and voice secret fears and vulnerabilities, they gradually were able to welcome and embrace each other in a way they never had before. This in turn encouraged them to open themselves more and more to each other, and a flourishing one-flesh bond began to grow.

Don't be misled. Nothing magic happened, and Pete and Jean didn't walk from their last session into a flawlessly happy-ever-after. They still had plenty of work to do in their marriage and in their family. But now they were doing it together. Rather than having only a rock-hard commitment to fall back on (and to bruise themselves on), they now had a life-giving awareness that they were truly part *of* each other and *for* each other.

Beyond Commitment

It is not uncommon to mistake *commitment to marriage*—sticking to your promise to be faithful and stay with your spouse—for *bonding in marriage*. We Christians often teach the Scripture's commands to be faithful in marriage as if they were the bottom line. We're right to uphold those commands, but if we stop there, we are missing the substance of marriage, the bond that makes that faithfulness both possible and joyful.

To some extent, we make the mistake out of ignorance, not fully realizing that a bonding of two lives is possible. We may have seen it demonstrated so rarely that we assume that when it does happen, those couples' experience is unusual and beyond what we have a right to expect.

I suspect, though, that more often we stop short of realizing what marriage can be because we are afraid. To let our husband or wife enter deep into the recesses of our lives arouses long-forgotten fears of being found unworthy of love, of being left abandoned and alone. Better to have the structure of a relationship, no matter how hollow inside, than to experience the terrifying possibility of being cast aside. So our marriages endure, but we never discover the joyous abandonment of the one-flesh relationship intended by our Creator.

A Divine Institution

Marriage is not an arrangement we have dreamed up on our own, for the sake of comfort or convenience. It is not a result of cultural evolution. It is a gift that was given to us at the beginning of time by God Himself. It was the crowning event of His acts of creation.

After He created the universe and the earth, the atmosphere and the landscape, living plants and animals, and a human being into whom He breathed His own life and graced with His image, God surveyed His work and declared it good. The account of creation and its goodness runs unbroken from Genesis 1:1 until the middle of Genesis 2 when, suddenly, God pronounced something "not good." He looked at Adam in the Garden, surrounded by living creatures but unable to commune with any of them, and He said, "It is not good for man to be alone. I will make a helper suitable for him."

What was it about Adam's being alone that was not good? Was it simply that he might have had a hard time managing the work of the Garden by himself? Some have drawn that conclusion from the fact that God proposed a "helper" for Adam.

But to think of God creating Eve merely as a convenience for Adam is to misunderstand not only the Creation story but also the nature of the universe and of God Himself. The world God had formed was not merely material and practical; it was also personal and relational, as He is. God, who is love, longs always to love and be loved in return, to give of Himself and to fellowship with another. When God declared that His creation was "good," He was saying that it was consistent with His character; the only thing that ran counter to His character was Adam's loneliness. In a world breathed into being from the depths of a loving God, the man made in His image needed someone to love and to be loved by in return.

So the Lord God caused the man to fall into a deep sleep; and while he was sleeping, He took one of the man's ribs and closed up the place with flesh. Then the Lord God made a woman from the rib He had taken out of the man, and He brought her to the man.

The man said, "This is now bone of my bones and flesh of my flesh; she shall be called 'woman,' for she was taken out of man."

For this reason a man will leave his father and mother and be united to his wife, and they will become one flesh.

The man and his wife were both naked, and they felt no shame (Genesis 2:21-25).

I don't know if Adam was aware of his deep need for another person. It may have slowly dawned on him as he named all the other creatures in the Garden and discovered in none of them a helper suitable for him.

Whatever his awareness of need, there is no mistaking his cry of recognition at its fulfillment: "This is now bone of my bones and flesh of my flesh!" It was a cry of mingled joy, relief, and satisfaction. Here, at last, was one with whom he could identify, with whom he could share his deepest thoughts and feelings and find understanding. Here was one with whom he could be united, not only physically but emotionally and spiritually, at the deepest level of his being. Here was someone to whom he could belong, and who could belong to him, permanently.

In reflecting on this passage, the Apostle Paul discovered in the one-flesh design of marriage a "mystery" (Ephesians 5:32)—the mystery of Christ's relationship with the church. The union that grows out of a man's and woman's need for each other is a living metaphor of God's relationship, through Christ, with His people. Embedded in the reality of Adam's need for Eve is the astounding fact that God has allowed Himself to want a relationship with *us*. In His greatness and self-sufficiency, He ordained a relationship in which He would participate. Although God is complete without us, He involves Himself on a personal level with His creation and is hurt if we don't respond.

It is a strange and beautiful eccentricity of the free God that He has allowed His heart to be emotionally identified with men. Self-sufficient as He is, He wants our love and will not be satisfied till He gets it. Free as He is, He has let His heart be bound to us forever.[1]

Relationship is at the heart of creation, because it is at the heart of who God is. The members of the Trinity have always been in perfect, loving, harmonious fellowship and interaction with each other. That interrelationship is so fundamental to who God is that it is impossible to conceive of Father, Son, or Holy Spirit existing or acting independently of the others—as impossible as imagining that your hands or feet could separate themselves from the rest of your body and carry on a life of their own.

Made in the image of God, we are made to relate to others. We don't really have a choice about that. We may try to deny our need for relationships, but it can't work. The most determined hermit, if he were honest, would at least have to acknowledge that at one time his very survival depended on having someone care for him.

To deny our need for relationships is to set ourselves up as superior to God and to defy the whole plan of creation. To strive to be self-sufficient, to be alienated from God and others, to be blind to our need for relationship—such pseudo-independence is the core of evil. It was the essence of Satan's rebellion against God when he declared that he would set up his own throne, independent of the Most High, and make himself a god above God (Isaiah 14:13-14). Of course, all he achieved was endless alienation and eternal defeat, and not a shred of real independence.

Accepting our need to be related to God and to others, we find that in marriage we may participate in the most potentially intimate human relationship possible; and in doing so, we affirm the chief ethic of creation. We acknowledge that we are not complete in and of ourselves and we allow ourselves to be vulnerable enough to give and receive love.

In Genesis 3 we read of man's fall into sin and the estrangement that ensued. Man and woman were alienated from each other and from God. Yet against all the ravages of sin, the institution of marriage survived and still stands as both a gift and vehicle of what some call "common grace," the goodness God gives to all men regardless of their relationship with Him. It is a continuing means by which two human beings can work at overcoming sin's divisive effects. Every marriage that survives is to some extent a victorious affirmation: "We are not alien to each other; we belong to one another." No wonder God chose marriage as an illustration of redemption. Redemption involves the constant reality that the relationship *is*.

Because of this I am distressed by the increasing ease and frequency of divorce in our society. Divorce not only strikes at the heart of who we are; it also violates the truth of God's created universe. Marriage is intended to be permanent, a relationship that we can rely on to be there. That permanence has nothing to do with legal or religious codes but with how we are made and what we need in order to live effectively.

I believe this need for marriage to be permanent resides in all of us. In my practice I do not see people coming to me in hope of finding a way to dissolve their marriage. Instead, they come to me with the agony of the rupture that has occurred in their relationship, seeking a way to heal it. Because marriage has been built into God's design for life itself, I believe that more often than not, healing is possible. But it requires a couple's willingness to understand and accept themselves as humans who need each other, and to give whatever is required to put new life into their marriage.

Bonding Inside and Out

In the 1980s, *bonding* became something of a catchword. The attention this term has received reflects a basic human hunger that has not been satisfied in the past quarter century of searching out new ways of living and relating to each other. Young people in the '60s looked at their parents' marriages and judged them hollow. What followed were years of trying to live and love apart from traditional structures and devising alternative lifestyles in a search for an authentic, satisfying relationship.

But the new structures have not proved any more fulfilling than the old ones, and the big news as we enter the last decade of the twentieth century is that marriage and family—in the traditional understanding of those terms—are back in. The number of marriages in 1987 was up six percent over the previous ten years—the sixth highest rate in U.S. history. We've tried structure, unstructure, new structures, and now we're back to the traditional in our search for a meaningful connection with another human being.

Yet I would be more heartened by the cultural swing toward marriage were it not for the fact that divorces are also occurring at a steady rate. Those who study such statistics tell us that in our society we can expect that half the marriages entered into will be dissolved in divorce.

So the structure of marriage, in itself, is not the solution. What answers our need is the kind of bonding that is possible only in marriage.

That is not to say, however, that structure should be ignored or discarded. It's tempting to think of bonding as something magical, and to want to pursue it apart from the structures that have disappointed us. That, in part, is what the variety of living arrangements of the past twenty-five years has been about. But just as human life requires a structure—a body—to contain, express, and empower it, so the life of a marriage must be embodied in order to survive.

Marriage, in its most basic structure, is a contract, an agreement between a man and a woman who want to form a lasting union. In entering into this agreement, they say to each other, "The primary allegiance I once gave to the family I was born into, I now give to you. I expect you to do the same and not to betray my loyalty. As marriage partners, we will have rights and privileges with each other that we will allow to no one else."

In our society, marriage is a legal contract which should stand for the *emotional contract* that has been made between a man and a woman. Some may dismiss the legal agreement as "just a piece of paper," as if it were unnecessary and irrelevant. But we need that piece of paper. We need a public acknowledgment that says yes, we have indeed agreed to commit ourselves to each other. The legal agreement is important because it expresses the value and seriousness of our emotional commitment to each other.

If the legal and emotional contract is the skeletal structure of a marriage, commitment and responsibility flesh out that structure. The marriage contract says, "I am committed to you above all others. All that I am and have, I will share with you. No matter what happens, I will not walk away from you. I agree to do my part toward making our relationship endure and grow. I am willing to shoulder whatever that involves." Unless that commitment is lived out daily, the contract is meaningless.

Flesh and bones alone do not constitute life, however, and a marriage constructed only of contractual obligations is lifeless indeed. If *contract* and *commitment* give form to a marriage, *bonding* is the soul of marriage, giving it life and meaning.

Bonding is that process by which a man and woman become "one flesh." It is the growing reality that this other person and I have become a part of each other. To separate would cause a pain so wrenching that we cannot even consider it as an option.

The Beginning of the Bond

How does it happen? Where does it begin? If you are married you can probably remember what it felt like to fall in love. Suddenly you could not bear to think about living without this other person. You *had to have* him or her. Together, your joy was complete; no one else mattered. Apart, you suffered an agony of longing until you were reunited. That deep certainty at the core of your being, "This one is for me!" echoed Adam's joyful exclamation when he first saw Eve.

That's where it begins. But it doesn't stop there. The intense need that gives birth to the bond develops into the secure knowledge, "We belong together. I'm safe with this person. He (or she) loves me and will not leave me. I'm free to reveal who I am." And little by little, a freedom of sharing grows, as the two of you reveal deeper and deeper aspects of yourselves. This freedom in sharing yourself and learning more and more about the other person is exciting and deeply satisfying. As it grows, so does the depth of your love for each other.

Thunder in Eden

Gradually, though, something disturbing creeps in—the awareness that this other person is *not* exactly like you. There are differences—some of them quite large. Those differences are unavoidable. They arise from the differences in your families' backgrounds, as expressed in lifestyle and values.

What's more, this other person has faults! Many of those faults, also, can be traced back to the individual's family. In a fallen world, none of us has had a perfect upbringing. Our parents raised us while they were trying to work out problems handed on to them by *their* parents.

A subtle panic may grow: "What if we're not perfect for each other, after all? What if I'm left alone again?"

At this point, there are two choices. You can hush the rising doubts, turn a blind eye to the differences, and doggedly cling to the heady feelings of being in love—and in the process set yourselves up for a crash later on. Or together you can face the differences and even the flaws, revise your pictures of each other and of the relationship according to what you now know is really there, and come anew to the declaration, "I love you exactly as you are. I accept even your differences. And I believe in your love for me—especially since you now know about ways in which I am different from you and imperfect."

In recognizing and accepting each other's individuality, the marriage bond has a chance to grow stronger, opening the way to a new depth of communication and sharing.

In a healthy marriage, the bond seems to grow in two directions at once: the husband and wife become closer and closer in their one-flesh unity, and at the same time they become more and more distinct as individuals. Because they are being loved and accepted for who they are, they have no need to deny their differences in order to please.

How do you experience the marriage bond? You feel it as you increasingly cherish one another for the differences as well as the likenesses. You experience it as you celebrate your unity through sexuality. You enjoy and nurture it as you spend time talking, listening, and responding to each other.

The bonding experience is an urgent need to share, and a shedding of the need to have secrets. It's the disquiet that comes if a problem isn't solved, the pain inside if something goes awry and isn't worked out between you. It's the joy of knowing and being known, the utter security of being yourself and belonging.

Marriage bonding is a process. It doesn't happen in an instant. And there are pitfalls along the way, which no couple avoids completely. But it is also a joyful possibility for the couple willing to take the risk.

Bonding: Letting Someone Else Inside

T he popular comic strip *Cathy* ran a series chronicling the pregnancy of Cathy's best friend, Andrea. One strip opened with Andrea lying on the couch with a tape recorder, headphones straddling her bulging belly, as Cathy and Cathy's mother looked on. Answering their quizzical expressions, Andrea explained that she was trying to help create a mother-child bond by playing a recording of her voice through the headphones to her unborn baby.

"Andrea," Cathy replied, "my mother never did that, and look at us." She went on to describe how she depended on her mother's approval, begged for her advice, ran to her for comfort, and in fact (here her face registered panic) could not make it though a week without calling her mother at least seventy-five times.

As Cathy's mother chimed in, "We're not bonded, we're crazy-glued!" Andrea clicked off the tape recorder.

Perhaps you know married couples who are "crazy-glued," so involved with each other they scarcely know who they are without the other partner to give them a frame of reference. And you probably know other couples who seem more like barely acquainted roommates than married lovers. Chances are, those marriages are very similar to the relationships the spouses had with their parents.

When we fall in love, as novel and exciting as we may find it, what we are experiencing is not as new and unique as we might think. In many ways, we are actually recapitulating a process that took place during the earliest days, months, and years of our lives. Our own particular, unique ways of loving are rooted in our infancy, when we fell in love for the first time. Our ways of loving grew from our great need to be loved and cared for, and our responses to the ones who filled that need.

As newborns, we knew nothing about what a relationship was, so what we learned with parents or other caretakers became a sort of universal truth for us. The bonds that were formed then became a pattern from which all our subsequent relationships were formed.

Bonding in Infancy and Early Childhood
Before we were born, we felt ourselves to be one with our mother's body. We were held, warmed, carried, and nourished by the womb that surrounded us, as if by magic. No wishes, demands, or efforts were required on our part.

Our passage through the birth canal did little to change that sense of ourselves, but birth brought with it an onslaught of new sensations. Lights, movement of air across our skin, sounds unmuffled by the womb, firm surfaces and myriads of hands to hold and support us, as well as a host of new internal sensations such as hunger, thirst, and fatigue, dramatically changed our newborn environment.

An infant has no understanding of the fact that he is now outside the mother, that he and his environment are not one, or that the demands of his body do not control his universe. In the womb he was omnipotent; now he is utterly dependent. His needs no longer control the universe, and he has no verbal means to make those needs known or to communicate pain or pleasure. Fortunately, he has no inkling of the potential desperateness of his plight.

His mother does know, and responds, in most cases, with a rush of tenderness, caring, and pleasure that have been mounting within her for nine months, just waiting to be released. Unless there was some serious lack in her own infancy or childhood, she senses these feelings very early in her newborn's life. It is a joy to cuddle, caress, feed, and gaze on this new person she and her husband have produced. The communication between parent and child is not in words but skin to skin. Her touch is the language he responds to as she attends to his every whimper and move, trying to anticipate his needs.

She is overwhelmed by the strength of the love she feels for this tiny being; although it has done nothing to earn her love, she knows she would willingly die for it. Her need to love and give is almost as great as the child's absolute need of her, and the child responds to her demonstrations of love with a sort of love of his own.

> *The Need and Need-love of the young is obvious; so is the Gift-love of the mother. She gives birth, gives suck, gives protection. On the other hand, she must give birth or die. She must give suck or suffer. That way, her Affection too is a Need-love. There is the paradox. It is a Need-love but what it needs is to give. It is a Gift-love but it needs to be needed.*[2]

The nurture provided by a good mother for her baby binds them tightly to each other and, in some ways, prolongs a womblike existence for the child. He feels hungry, cries, and is fed. He sleeps and wakes up, uncomfortable from being in one position too long. He cries and is picked up and cuddled and rocked. He breathes the reassuring smell of his mother's body, is stilled by the increasingly familiar tones of her voice. His wishes and needs still seem to have the power to bring him comfort.

At least they do most of the time. But sometimes Mother

is tired or busy and does not come right away. Sometimes he is held and cuddled but not fed the moment he declares his hunger. And sometimes, no matter how much he cries, his wish goes unfulfilled as Mother puzzles in vain over what might be the problem.

During the first weeks of life, a baby gradually discovers that Mother is *outside* of him (although he still perceives her "outsideness" as an extension of himself, which he controls through his needs). As the baby's central nervous system develops, so does his capacity for realizing the distinction between himself and his mother. By the age of two weeks he can smile when her face appears over the side of his crib. Later he discovers his fingers and feet, and the fact that he can move them at will and, in time, he begins to understand where his body leaves off and Mother's begins.

At the same time that Mother's separateness is dawning on him, though, a sense of trust and security is growing to fill her place when she is absent. Rather than feeling desperate and abandoned, he expects that Mother will reappear and that he can cope and soothe himself until she does. The warmth and love he receives from her flood his body and remain with him for longer and longer periods of time when she is gone.

By the time he is old enough to walk he carries his nurturing mother "inside" of him. Through internalizing her caring responses to his coos, cries, and smiles, he becomes grounded in a sense of self and security in a basically safe world.

Meanwhile, his parents are delighting in the almost constant changes taking place as he grows. His first smile, his eyes lighting with recognition when they appear, the way his gaze follows their faces around the room, his first labored attempts at pulling himself across the floor—all are met with joy and increasing wonder as they get to know this new person in their family.

Although they recognize Father's eyes and Mother's chin,

they realize more and more that in very important ways he is different from either of them. He is unique, becoming more and more his own person. And if his parents are secure in themselves, they celebrate his uniqueness and respond with delight to his being himself. He learns from them that it is okay to be who he is. His differences from his parents will not cut off the supply of their love. Filled and contented with that love, he increases in security and courage to grow and discover more of himself and his world with each new day.

As he grows in his individuality, his bond to his parents is strengthened. As he takes his first lurching steps across the room and then ventures further afield, he knows Mother and Father will be there for him to come back to if the territory becomes too unfamiliar. It's okay to go and okay to come back again, because he is filled with a sense that both he and the nurturing parents he now carries inside of him are okay.

Bonding Gone Awry

The simultaneous growth of self-discovery and of bonding to parents is an intricate process, a delicate interplay between parents and child. And it is fraught with potential for going awry. Not since Adam's fall has there been a perfect parent—or, for that matter, a perfect baby (except Jesus).

Sometimes a child, for organic reasons, becomes autistic, unable to absorb the love and stimulation his parents give him. He remains in the closed world of infancy, in a world of his own, not perceiving his own self or others. He may never be able to come out from behind the locked doors and interact with the environment around him.

Sometimes a mother is absent or, because of problems stemming from her own background, is angry or indifferent toward her child and doesn't give him the nurturance he needs in order to grow healthily. In the face of ill treatment, he withdraws into himself. Met with abandonment or indifference, he loses interest in life and fails to thrive.

Psychologist René Spitz described this phenomenon in detail after observing infants in foundling homes after World War II. Although all their physical needs were met—they were adequately fed, clothed, and bathed—they fussed and cried for several weeks, and then, as if giving up, they became quiet and withdrawn. Many failed physically and became increasingly inactive at an age when other infants grow stronger and begin to reach out to the world around them. A number of them showed symptoms of malnutrition and even died.

The key to their condition lay not in the physical but in the emotional care they were receiving. The caretaking staff was efficient, but the babies outnumbered them by about eight to one. Consequently, most of the babies were touched only when they were fed, clothed, or bathed, and were rarely held. They were often not even held while being fed; instead, their bottles were propped beside them to free the nurse to move on to the next crying child. There was no time to cuddle, rock, or caress the children. No one sang lullabies to them or smiled into their eyes. No one was *there* for them.

Without someone to bond with—to be loved by and to respond to, to become part of them, to let them know that they and the world were okay—the babies could not go on. Life became unlivable.

The situation René Spitz found was extreme, as were its effects on the babies involved. However, similar effects can be seen whenever a baby is cut off from a nurturing figure during the time he needs to be bonding with one.

Between the ages of three and nine months a child needs a consistent nurturing figure with whom to bond. If the bonding process is interrupted during that time—for instance, if the child is taken from a foster home and placed with an adoptive family—the rupture in the bonding may remain with the child throughout life. The child carries a hidden longing that is never filled and that can resurface later, especially during adolescence.

Jenny was such a child. Because of complications surrounding her birth, Jenny was not healthy during the first months of her life. Debbie, her teenage mother, felt fearful, at first, about her original decision to put the baby up for adoption. What if an adoptive family would not give Jenny the love and care she needed?

But as the baby grew, she gained strength; and her mother, although she was growing more and more attached to Jenny, was also finding it more and more difficult to care for her alone. Finally, she gave up, and when the child was seven months old, Debbie placed Jenny with an adoptive family. She had agonized over the decision—she could hardly bear the thought of Jenny not living with her anymore—but she believed that Jenny would be better off in a stable, two-parent family.

As attached as Debbie was to Jenny, Jenny was even more attached to Debbie, and she did not take well to her new family. She cried and fussed continually, and grew even more fretful when strange hands picked her up and unfamiliar arms rocked her. As her frustration grew, so did that of her new mother and father, who were beginning to doubt their abilities as parents. They handled her gingerly, fearful of making a wrong move. It was some time before the three of them eventually settled into a tenuous rapport with each other.

As Jenny grew, she seemed relatively happy with her new family, but her adoptive parents sometimes experienced a vague disappointment that Jenny did not seem as attached to them as they had expected a child to be.

It was when Jenny was a teenager, though, that the real trouble began. Always seemingly self-sufficient, Jenny became depressed and suicidal. She complained of feeling unloved and not belonging anywhere, and no reassurances of love from her parents seemed to have any effect.

In reality, those reassurances *had* no effect, because they couldn't reach down to the place where she was really hurting. They couldn't fill the hole that was left when she had been separated from her biological mother. Since babyhood she had unconsciously been longing for that original bond, and had never been able to allow another bond to replace it. She had never allowed herself to feel fully loved by her new family, and, sensing their disappointment, she had always carried an unconscious belief that there was something intrinsically wrong with her that had caused her to be rejected in the first place and now prevented her from loving or being loved.

Jenny's symptoms, in varying degrees, can be present in any child, adopted or not, who was unable to bond adequately as an infant. Sometimes a mother is physically or emotionally unable to provide all the nurturance an infant needs; sometimes she is hindered by circumstances. Any gaps that occur in the bonding process remain with the child unless later experience with a nurturing person can provide some healing.

Just as too early a separation or too little nurturing during a child's first year can disrupt the bonding process, so failure to gain a healthy independence during the second and third year of life can thwart the purpose of bonding. Sometimes a mother, because of unmet needs in her own life, is unable to let go of her child and encourage him in his growing individuality. Rather than enjoying this stage in his development, she misses being the star around which his universe revolves. Subtly she communicates the message that, if he wants to be loved, her child will not leave her, not become different from her, not grow in self-confidence but remain dependent on her. He learns, in an unconscious but powerful way, "I'm here to serve Mother's needs. If I don't, I will lose her. I will be abandoned." The clinging relationship that results may look like closeness, but in reality it is a sophisticated form of rejection: the child is not allowed to be himself.

Kenny was born to a woman who was frustrated and lonely in her marriage to a workaholic. She lavished love and attention on him and made him the center of her world. As a result, he didn't grow away, in preschool years, from having her be the center of *his* world. He seldom strayed from his own yard and clung anxiously to his mother rather than join in the play of the other toddlers at the park. When he started school, he was shy and awkward with other children, and he would hurry home to bask in the seemingly unlimited approval and warmth of his mother.

As he entered his teen years, rather than identify with a group of peers, as would be normal, Kenny became more and more of a loner. He blushed and fumbled for words if any of his classmates spoke to him, particularly if they were girls. He longed to be part of the group but was at a loss to know how to connect with others.

His mother flew to his rescue. To save him from his social struggles and embarrassment, she found reasons for him not to join in school and social activities, telling him she needed him at home. Her apparent need for him was hard to resist—but so was his inner need to forge his own identity and relationships outside his home.

The dilemma was unresolvable. He dealt with it by escaping into drugs, which gave him an illusion of freedom and masked his loneliness.

In an imperfect world, we all tend to fall on one side or the other of the perfect bonding experience. None of us completely escapes the pitfalls of growing. None of us has been loved perfectly; none of us has had the opportunity to trust absolutely; none of us carries perfect parent images inside.

But most of us receive some measure of what we need to enable us to grow, to make lives of our own, and to form relationships along the way. The bond with our parents continues with us as a blueprint for all future relationships. The kind of trust in ourselves and others that we learned back in early childhood determines the quality of trust we bring to all our interactions with others. Nowhere is this seen more clearly than in marriage.

Choosing a Mate

In biblical times the connection between one's bond with his or her parents and the choice of a mate was fairly concrete: parents chose the mate. We Westerners may shake our heads in wonder that marriages in those days survived. We might even roll our eyes at the thought of what kind of mate we might have ended up with if our marriages had been arranged.

There is little documentation in Scripture as to whether those marriages were "successful." We know that many of them lasted, while others did not (as demonstrated by Moses' need to establish a procedure for divorce). How did the patriarchs do it? How did marriages not founded on romance last?

Actually those marriages may not have faced the level of risk we imagine. Although not necessarily based on romantic love, they *were* based on the bond between parents and child. To the extent that that bond was healthy, with the parents unselfishly loving the child and seeking his best interests, we may guess that the son's or daughter's needs and feelings were taken into account in the choice of a mate. In addition, most Hebrews were careful to choose a child's mate from within their own culture, not from the pagan nations surrounding them. Many parents searched only within their own extended families, as Abraham instructed his servant to do for Isaac (Genesis 24:3-5).

Although arranged marriages seem a bit artificial to us, they apparently could be as fulfilling as any in our culture. Scripture tells us that Isaac, grieving after his mother's death, was comforted in his newfound love for Rebekah (Genesis 24:67). As the longed-for only son of his parents, and the fulfillment of God's promises to them, Isaac did not lack for parental love and attention. Sarah apparently doted on the boy (Genesis 21:8-10), and this relationship may well have been the springboard for Isaac's successful bonding with his wife. Although their marriage developed problems, especially in later years, they stayed together

(Isaac didn't even add a second wife, as was common in that day) and raised the progenitors of two great nations.

Although families in our society do not arrange children's marriages, parents play a far larger role in the choice of a partner than we at first might think. Even at a surface level, a son or daughter often judges a prospective mate by the criterion, "What would Mother or Father think?" Spoken and unspoken messages from parents about what is desirable help direct the search for the ideal partner.

In addition, the relationship we saw between Mother and Father helps us make decisions—conscious and unconscious—about what we do and do not want in our own marriage. Sometimes we want to repeat what we saw. Sometimes we want to undo it, and so will search for a partner who seems to promise the opposite experience.

Underneath the model and messages we received from our parents are all the emotional needs we have carried with us from infancy that spur us on to find our "missing pieces" in another. At that deeper level, the often unconscious memories of our earliest love object play a powerful role in our choice of a marriage partner. It is as if forgotten longings for oneness with another are again stirred up as we enter young adulthood. Though we don't plan it consciously, we seek for that one with whom we can find the same level of satisfaction we enjoyed in babyhood.

When that one is found, something clicks; the missing pieces seem to slide into prearranged spaces. As acquaintance ripens into love, the intensity of our feeling for each other mirrors the intense need-love between a mother and her child. For the time being, the rest of the world is forgotten; all that matters is that the two of us have each other. We look only to each other for the fulfillment of all our hopes and longings.

At this early stage, some couples jump prematurely into a sexual relationship, mistakenly believing that sex will seal their bond with each other. But reducing the bond to a sexual relationship short-circuits the process of developing the deep emotional union that sexuality is meant to celebrate. A healthy, intimate bond is not given the chance to develop. Without that, sex becomes merely a sharing of bodies rather than a true sharing of selves. When Adam welcomed Eve as "bone of my bone and flesh of my flesh," he was not referring to just the possibility of a sexual relationship. His words pointed beyond the physical relationship to the union of two souls, two complete persons meeting and welcoming each other into their lives.[3]

Bypassing the bond leaves us stuck. Sex for its own sake is a snare, entangling us with each other but not meeting our heart needs for intimacy. So we become compulsive, driven to try again and again to make it "work," but we gain only temporary relief. Instead of enjoying sexual freedom, we feel trapped and impoverished.

True sexual freedom requires soul-level intimacy. When an intimate bond is developing from the inside out, sex no longer carries the compulsion to reassure oneself of closeness; it becomes the free expression that the two *are* one— or at least are growing in oneness. A sexual relationship begun before marriage is rarely as satisfying as one that is enjoyed totally within a committed partnership.

After the Choice
Just as the infant must gradually recognize the difference between himself and his mother, so those newly in love must gradually accept each other's separateness. Our relationship with our mate deepens as we are each willing to take even tentative steps into unknown territory—revealing parts of ourselves previously unknown to the other, and receiving disclosures of the other's unseen self.

Intimacy depends on the fact that the two of us *are* different. That is why we need each other. As we share our differences and needs—as risky as that can feel—the bond between us grows stronger.

Intimacy is not just letting somebody else know what I

need. It is letting him or her know things about me that reveal a need too hard to voice, and sharing that exquisitely sensitive something that could give the other person the opportunity to destroy me.

Intimacy is letting that other person inside me. It is a growing recognition that this other one is *for* me, whether or not my wishes and needs are always met in the way that I want. In marriage, as in childhood, we learn to move from the position, "I can change the world just by wishing," to the realization that it is the character of the other that counts, not the perfection with which he or she can perform. It is the intention of the heart: Does he care? Not, does he fail me? but, how does he *feel* when he fails me? Do I dare to be vulnerable enough to find out and to discover whether the relationship is still there?

As I begin to carry the other "inside" me, I learn that I can voice my secret fears and failings and know that they will be accepted not with judgment but with support; not with answers but with the assurance that my spouse believes in me and trusts in my wish to change for the better, even when I seem to be floundering.

Bonding depends on my willingness to communicate who I am, and on my partner's ability to draw my secrets out of me when I am holding back. It is a process of testing, taking step after tentative step with each other. Can I overcome my fears of rejection and say what I am thinking? Can I be clear and forthright rather than camouflaging my real meaning? Will what I say be understood? And can I get beyond the surface facts and let the feelings follow—whether hurt, fear, anguish, or joy?

Each time we go through this process, it is a turning point, a sort of crisis in the development of our relationship. And each time we face and overcome a threat to our esteem, each time we acknowledge and resolve a problem, we reconfirm and deepen our bond. Romance and infatuation that are untested by the onslaught of differences are not sufficient to create a bond. Marriage gains strength and endurance through the rigors of willfully trusting each other against all odds.

Fear of Intimacy

Oneness is a process that is often painful and never complete. There is a tremendous risk in letting ourselves be known. Not since before the Fall have humans experienced being "naked and not ashamed." Alienation runs deep—our alienation from God resulting in our alienation from ourselves and each other. While we may not always admit that we are sinners, we *know* that we are. That knowledge feeds our fear that if we are known, we will be blamed, punished, or abandoned.

So out of fear we try always to guard our innermost selves from exposure. But when we do that, we cut ourselves off from the very solution to our alienation. The walls that protect us from rejection also protect us from the joy of being accepted, of knowing that when we open up the areas of our lives where we are hurting and vulnerable, we can be cared for.

When couples harbor secrets from each other, they prevent their bond from becoming complete. Or, having once heard the other's secret, a spouse will tell it to someone outside the marriage as a way of saying, "I'm not willing to commit myself to this depth of intimacy."

People who feel the need to reveal themselves at a deeper level may share their secrets with someone other than their spouse. At its extreme, this practice results in an extramarital affair—a way to have their cake and eat it too. The affair feels safe because by its very nature it is not permanent and does not require commitment—and therefore does not entail the same risk of betrayal or abandonment. If they get burned, there is a back door of escape.

Overcoming the Fear

We submit ourselves to the dangers of intimacy because we cannot help ourselves. Try as we might, we cannot escape our God-given need to belong to someone. The alternative is aloneness, that "not good" condition. Only those who have been badly damaged by others truly want to be alone. We *need* to have another person inside.

When a couple comes to me with a marriage that is in trouble, I try to tap into that need. I seek to help each spouse get behind the smokescreen of problems with finances or children and back to that wish to belong to each other. When a marriage benefits from counseling, it is because the individuals have been able to get in touch with their heart desire for each other and have chipped away at the fears that have blocked that desire.

Scripture's Endorsement of the Marriage Bond

Our marriages are as imperfect as we are. Yet Scripture gives marriage a place of honor that outranks any other earthly relationship. No other human relationship is given as many endorsements or safeguards (see Genesis 2:24; Exodus 20:14; Deuteronomy 7:3; Matthew 19:4-6; 1 Corinthians 6:15-16; 7:1-16; 2 Corinthians 6:14; Hebrews 13:4).

Marriage symbolizes God's bond with His people (Hosea 2:16, 19-20; Ephesians 4:21-32; Revelation 21:2, 9). That fact alone makes marriage worthy of the care given to it in Scripture. Yet by the grace of God, the hedges He has set up around marriage are not primarily for His benefit but for our own. Obedience to biblical instructions concerning marriage leads us into a deeper understanding and richer experience of our relationship with Christ. It also provides the setting in which we can best satisfy our deepest human needs.

When the marriage bond is meeting the needs it was designed to satisfy, husband and wife are free to nurture children in ways that allow them to grow into the kind of bonding experience they need to be confident and to form healthy attachments. Because the marriage is secure, the children may feel safe in depending on their parents and in venturing out on their own. And so the cycle continues.

t h r e e

Love: The Tie That Bonds

After fourteen years of marriage and three children, Julia looked across the breakfast table at her husband, Paul, absorbed in *The Wall Street Journal*, and realized the only emotion she felt toward him was a generalized irritation. She was bored with their perfunctory conversation, tired of his annoying habits, and resentful of his demands on her. And as far as she could tell, he was no happier with her than she was with him.

She had been aware of these feelings, with varying degrees of intensity, for some time. This morning they were hitting her full force. Julia and Paul had just returned from a week's visit with her sister and her family, and she had been struck by how genuinely happy her sister and brother-in-law were with each other. She was so accustomed to the friction between herself and Paul that her sister's happiness caught her by surprise. She had forgotten that married people could actually enjoy each other that much.

So this morning, instead of just accepting her feelings as normal to those past the honeymoon stage, she started asking herself some questions. Where had these bad feelings come from? When had they started? How were they different from what she had felt during their courtship? On their wedding day? During their first year of marriage? What had changed? Did she and Paul love each other now? Had they ever—really? If they had (and certainly, they had thought so when they married), what had happened to that love? Had it entirely disappeared, or was it buried somewhere in the dust and debris that had settled over their lives?

Many people, when they start asking such questions, move quickly to a negative conclusion. If the good feelings aren't there now, perhaps they never really were; or even if they existed once, they seem to be permanently gone now. So now what? Many decide that divorce is the next step, and will even tell you that it's the right and caring thing to do. I have known of some Christians, faced with a seemingly loveless marriage, who conclude that it must not have been God's will for them to have married their spouse in the first place, that they had been misguided or ignorant in doing so—and that they should therefore not stay with this person.

What these couples don't realize, or don't want to accept, is that it's too simplistic to say,

"Marriage − Love = No Point in Staying Together."

For one thing, they usually aren't defining their terms well. What is marriage to them? Even more important, what do they mean by *love*?

To deal with a deficit in our lives by subtracting still more doesn't make good sense. It is much better to find what is missing, with the hope that the equation can balance out. Granted, this isn't always possible, and divorces will happen. But I never advise divorce, and I'm undauntedly hopeful, no matter how many statistics you show me, that couples whose emotions are operating in the red can yet find what is missing to make their relationships add up.

Julia was asking some good questions and, fortunately, she and Paul were both willing to take the long road to sorting out the answers, rather than by-passing the problems or taking the shortcut of divorce. The discomfort in their marriage prodded both of them to find what they had lost on their fourteen-year journey together.

As they explored their relationship, Julia and Paul discovered that they had indeed loved each other when they married. They also discovered that their love had in some ways been immature and unformed and that other factors—intense, emotional factors—had motivated them to choose and marry each other.

Not knowing what else to call these other factors at the time, and not being fully aware of their impact on the decision to marry, they had assumed that these were part of being "in love." Julia and Paul were both good-looking people who had met each other at an age when sexuality was at the forefront of their conscious and unconscious awareness. Each thought the other the most beautiful person they had ever seen, and they were head over heels from the moment they met. In addition, family factors intensified their feelings for each other. Paul had an uncomfortable home life he wanted to escape. Julia noticed that her parents were very impressed with Paul and encouraged her to include him in family outings. Her need to please her parents added strength to her attraction to Paul.

As they sorted through the motivations that drew them together, they discovered underneath them all a genuine caring and delight in each other. Putting other factors in their place allowed them the freedom to let go of yearning for the intense feelings those factors had generated and to welcome the solid, enduring feelings they held for each other. The fizz of infatuation was no longer theirs, but they were free to enjoy each other in ways that the pressures of infatuation wouldn't allow. Long gone was the relief of getting out from under his parents' roof, but now Paul could allow himself to appreciate the life he had with Julia. And now Julia could allow herself to delight in Paul for his own sake, not just because her parents had been pleased with him.

Barriers to Love

We were not born as loving creatures—indifferent as we were to anything outside of ourselves—but we did have the capacity to respond. As babies, we learned to give love by being on the receiving end. When we were loved, our response was first satisfaction, then gratitude, gradually trust, and finally love in return. That love was made up of all the feelings and attitudes we were developing toward those people we were beginning to carry inside ourselves. Love begins with need, but it does not stay needy. As our needs are filled, and we grow in trust and self-confidence, we find that we have a love to give back, and we become equal participants in the relationship. What begins as need-love becomes a giving-love that reaches out to the other and finds satisfaction when the object of love is satisfied.

However, the process of learning to love is never smooth. We live in a world riddled with alienation, and none of us is immune to its effects. Marriage dares to defy alienation, but in doing so it wages a battle against very real odds. We bring to marriage not just a desire to love and give ourselves to another but also a core of mistrust that has been reinforced by our life experiences.

• Double messages. In the broadest sense, what keeps us from feeling loved, and thus prevents us from freely giving love, are double messages—the experience of hearing one message but having it contradicted by other messages, verbal or nonverbal.

Jim's parents were busy people with important careers. He was told that he was loved; birthday cards and letters sent to him at summer camp were always signed, "Love, Mom and Dad." But the only times he received his parents' full attention was when he did something that annoyed or embarrassed them—and then, of course, the attention was negative. He carried within him an uneasy feeling that all was not well, that something was missing. Yet to question the reality of his parents' love for him brought condemnations of his "insensitivity" and "ingratitude." Confused, he

drove his questions underground. On the surface he complied with his parents' wishes, but inside he decided he
was on his own.

Because what we grow up with tends to feel normal to
us, Jim entered marriage not really even aware that he had
encountered double messages as a child. He assumed that
his experience with his parents was the way all relationships worked. Consequently, when his wife declared her
love for him, he responded with a polite but distant kind of
love of his own, but he never really entrusted himself to
her or expected her to cherish him as a person. He kept his
feelings to himself, especially when he was hurt. He never
truly opened himself to his wife's love, and therefore never
was able to give himself to her with abandon.

In another case, Mary received a different kind of double
message from her parents. Yes, she was loved, they told
her. But they expressed appreciation for her only when she
was excellent—only when she got straight A's, won awards
for her piano playing, kept her room immaculate, and
didn't express negative feelings such as anger or sadness.
Warmth and acceptance had stringent conditions. At an
emotional level she learned, "I am of value only when my
performance pleases my parents and serves their needs.
Who I am as a person is irrelevant."

Double messages are a very subtle form of emotional
abuse. They devalue the person as surely as physical or
sexual abuse does. Parents' emotional abuse of children—
using them for their own gratification—is not easily recognized or acknowledged by victim, perpetrator, or society.
Its effects, however, are as real as any experienced by
those who endure beatings or incest. The victim of abuse
comes to the almost unshakable conclusion that he or she
has no inherent value. The only hope of "love" lies in gratifying someone more powerful; and when that becomes
either impossible or intolerable, despair sets in.

The devastating personal effects of abuse have predict-
able results in marriage. In the first place, not seeing them-

selves as valuable or lovable, victims often marry someone who will perpetuate the abuse at some level. It is the only kind of relationship they have ever known or can conceive of. Or they will in turn abuse their partner or their children.

To be able to accept love, you must see yourself as worth being loved; to be able to give love, you must see your love as a desirable gift. Without that foundation, it is only with great difficulty, and often with professional help, that a person can learn to receive another's genuine caring or to give such caring himself.

• Inadequate experience. Some people enter marriage carrying barriers to being loved that stem from simple lack of experience. For some reason—whether illness, separation, death, or divorce—a parent's love was not available to them to the extent they needed. Having learned early that they could not depend on receiving care, they develop a defensive armor to protect themselves from the enticement of warmth. Or, conversely, they carry an insatiable hunger for love into all relationships, without being selective, and attach themselves suffocatingly to anyone they can find; but try as they will, they never seem to be able to feel loved. Either way, they miss out on a true experience of love.'

The Heart of the Matter

Our human experience of love is inadequate and faulty. But we are not left to flounder or guess at what love truly is. One of the best-known Scripture passages, Paul's great treatise on love in 1 Corinthians 13, describes the attitudes and actions by which love is known: "Love is . . . love does. . . ."

> *Love is patient, love is kind. It does not envy, it does not boast, it is not proud. It is not rude, it is not self-seeking, it is not easily angered, it keeps no record of wrongs. Love does not delight in evil but rejoices with the truth. It always protects, always trusts,*

always hopes, always perseveres. Love never fails
(1 Corinthians 13:4-8).

If you've ever tried to make that description true of your life and relationships, you know how difficult it is on a daily basis. At times you may succeed in acting loving, but sooner or later you find yourself harboring an attitude that is definitely not loving.

Left to our own resources, we often find our love to be in short supply. But Scripture tells us that the source of love is God Himself. The Apostle John wrote, "Dear friends, let us love one another, for *love comes from God* (1 John 4:7). We have on our side One who has promised to be a limitless resource as we seek to be truly loving.

With our human limitations, many of us tend to isolate pieces of love and take them for the whole. We say love is loyalty or affection or sex or endurance or an act of the will or performance of duty or romance. All these things teach us about love and are aspects of love, but they aren't all there is.

Love is an expression of one whole person toward another whole person. Scripture often uses the word *heart* to point to the essence of a person, the totality of the inner being. The heart cannot be broken down into neat, separate parts called thinking, feeling, and will; it includes each of those but they overlap and intermingle. In the same way, love, as an expression of the heart, is greater than its separate components. It is an expression of one total person reaching out to another.

Love implies the coming together of two people in such a way that they open themselves fully and share themselves with each other. They talk and listen, eager to be in touch with each other at the deepest level. In the process, all that they are—background, culture, preferences, and prejudices—is offered up to the other and becomes vulnerable to change. They connect with each other, respond to each other, affect each other—and they are never the same persons they were before they let each other into their lives. Love is not a vague, fuzzy, philosophical ideal but a vibrant, active interchange.

Love and Duty

A notion popular in some Christian circles is that love is not an emotion but an act of the will. Christ commanded love, they say; therefore, love is a duty to be performed, whether we feel like it or not.

While I understand and sympathize with the intent of that thinking, I'm not happy with the barrenness of the net result. Yes, we are called to love. But to reduce love to a *should* empties it of its true meaning. Duty is part of love but not the whole.

Does God love us out of a sense of duty, because it's something He *should* do? Does He yearn for intimate involvement in our lives only out of a sense of moral obligation?

Or does He love us because it is the fullest expression of who He is? "God is love," wrote John, the apostle who recognized himself as beloved (John 13:23; 19:26; 20:2; 21:7, 20). God's love for us flows from His heart, the depth and core of His being. In love, He actively seeks relationship with those He created *for* relationship. The Old Testament commands us to love God and neighbor (Leviticus 19:18, 34; Deuteronomy 6:5; 11:1, 13, 22), and Christ affirmed those commandments in His "new commandment" (John 13:34). But the commandments are not telling us merely to conjure up feelings or perform certain actions. They are invitations to abandon ourselves fully to being who we were created to be—expressing our humanness by giving ourselves to God and our neighbor and letting them into our lives.

That's the ideal. It calls us back to a state that existed before sin entered our world and tore relationships apart. The Gospel, the good news, says that because of Christ's death we can enjoy restored relationships with God and with each other. We are free to relate once again as whole people, giving from our hearts, as God conforms us to His own image (Romans 8:29). "We love because He first loved us" (1 John 4:19). That love is not performance split off from the essence of who we are; rather, it is the joyful expression of all that we are and welcomes others in their totality.

You may be saying, "That's lovely, but it sounds so abstract, so lofty, so *theological*. How can I make that kind of love happen in my day-to-day life?"

Marriage, because of its foundation of exclusiveness and permanence, is a uniquely safe place in which to participate in the kind of unity God intended for His people from the beginning. Day by day, you can choose to let your mate in on what you are thinking and feeling. You can speak rather than harbor hurt, resentment, fear, or disapproval. You can ask questions rather than remain confused by your spouse's actions or words. You can set aside your self-absorption and listen to what your mate tells you about his or her thoughts, feelings, wishes, and hopes. You can choose to consider thoughtfully the feedback he or she gives you about yourself, and also to accept the need for change when it arises. In marriage, more than in any other relationship, it is safe to do this because you belong to each other. And as you communicate this way, your commitment to each other is confirmed and breeds trust and love.

As my wife and I look back over our years of marriage, we realize that although we loved each other on our wedding day, that love was full of uncertainties we were unaware of at the time. It is from the vantage point of the solid security we feel with each other now that we can recognize, by contrast, the holes of mistrust our relationship had then. The process of living together, learning to know and be known by each other, solving problems together, and sharing innumerable experiences with each other has fed our love for each other and brought it to a maturity we could not have known at the outset.

That's the way married love is. Those who expect their love to be flawless the moment they are married are doomed to disappointment. Love grows with the deepening of the relationship.

By God's grace, even those who do not know Him may enjoy some measure of the unity He designed into marriage. For Christians, however, the potential for oneness increases as God is allowed to participate in the lives and relationship of husband and wife. To the extent that they understand how much they are loved and accepted by Him, they experience the freedom to venture into greater intimacy with each other.

Love at Its Best

The English language has only one word to denote all the variations of love. Most other languages are more precise. The Greek in which the New Testament was written had four words for love: *phileo*, the love between relatives and friends; *eros*, the passionate desire of a man and woman for each other; *stergo*, a natural affection, such as between a parent and child; and *agape*, which originally meant "to honor" or "to welcome."

In Scripture, *agape* is the word most often used for love. Both the New Testament and the Septuagint (the Greek translation of the Old Testament) use the term *agape* to describe the relationship between God and His people. *Agape* is a love that chooses to love and remains unshaken in its faithfulness and its desire for the good of the loved one. *Agape* originates in God Himself and calls forth a response of love from the loved one.

In Ephesians 5:22, Paul used the term *agape* in instructing husbands to love their wives as Christ loved the church. In marriage, husband and wife are to be bound by a covenant love for each other that is modeled after God's own love for His people.

Perhaps because *agape* appears frequently in Scripture,

and because it is used to describe God's love for His people, some have concluded that *agape* is the only "good" love, and other kinds of love are inferior or tainted. In marriage, *agape* love is essential. But so are *phileo* or friendship love, *stergo* or affectionate love, and *eros* or romantic, sexual love. Each kind of love needs the others, and all combined are the expression of the lovers' hearts.

I think it is especially important to remember this in regard to *eros*. Through the years, the church has often relegated *eros* to an inferior, if not sinful, status. But the writers of Scripture did not see it that way. Nowhere in the Bible is erotic love, per se, disparaged. The Prophet Hosea even pointed to the passionate love between husband and wife to convey to Israel the intensity of the Lord's desire for His people (Hosea 3:1). The writer to the Hebrews acknowledged the worthiness of romantic, sexual love by admonishing his readers to honor and protect the marriage bed (Hebrews 13:4).

But someone may object, "Isn't *eros* essentially selfish—and therefore sinful?" Is it? We may misuse *eros*, as well as the other kinds of love, to selfish ends; but is it, in itself, selfish? Was selfishness inherent in the romantic love God gave Adam and Eve for each other? I don't think so. *Eros*, as all our loves, was contaminated in the Fall. But in the beginning, *eros* was intended to be giving, not merely self-seeking. Even as sinners we can know some measure of the experience that sexual love is at its best when we are satisfying the loved one—when we are intent upon giving ourselves, not just gratifying our own desires.

C.S. Lewis observed, "The Divine Love [*agape*] does not *substitute* itself for the natural—as if we had to throw away our silver to make room for the gold. The natural loves are summoned to become modes of Charity while also remaining the natural loves they were."[4]

Our mate must be our friend, confidant, companion, and lover. All the loves are wrapped up together into a unifying whole, a celebration of the coming together of two people against the forces of alienation. "Love is as strong as death," rejoiced the sage. "Many waters cannot quench love; rivers cannot wash it away" (Song of Solomon 8:6-7). He was not talking about some philosophical ideal or moral obligation but about the marital love that goes on between two humans who have decided to give themselves to each other in every way.

When Love Has Gone
You may be reading this and thinking, "All this talk about love is fine for those who are just starting out, those who are still in love. But love has gone from my marriage. We don't love each other anymore."

My first question to you is, "What are you calling love?" Remember, Julia and Paul had lost many of the intense feelings that had been present when they first married. But they discovered that those feelings, spawned by a number of factors that motivated them to cling to each other, were not really love.

In other cases, couples may begin to feel that they are not in love anymore simply because they have gotten beyond their idealizations of each other and have discovered each other as real people. He's not Prince Charming; she's not Sleeping Beauty. The heady feelings they had as they entered their fairy-tale marriage do not withstand day-to-day life exposing who they are as individuals with very real differences.

Paradoxically, this disillusionment, this sense that love has evaporated in the strong light of reality, is a blessing. In the dissipation of romantic illusions, there is hope that now the two of you can really begin to know each other as people with attributes and needs that are unique and special.

Real love, instead of evaporating with exposure to the loved one, grows stronger and more substantial, so that years later husband and wife look at each other, shake their heads in wonder, and say, "We had no idea what love was when we married. The feelings we had for each other then barely scratched the surface compared to the love we share now."

Stand back and look at each other and ask, "What was it that drew us together in the first place? Who are we? What have we been to each other? What have we done with our desire to be together?" As you explore the answers to those questions, you can come to a new awareness of who you are and what your marriage has meant—and can mean—to you. In the process of knowing each other, love awakens.

It is, in many ways, a brand new awakening, not a re-awakening of love, and it brings new life to your marriage. The more you recognize and accept each other as real people, the more you open yourselves to the fulfillment of the needs behind your seeking and choosing each other in the first place.

Most of the couples who come to me for marital therapy, when they go back and look at what brought them together, do not split. They stay together because they discover something greater than all their problems—even when less-than-noble reasons such as escaping from home, parental pressure, or romantic idealization prompted their marriage. They discover a heart need for each other that goes deeper than those reasons. And in that discovery, they find the ability and desire to accept each other now, differences and all.

Burnout or Cop-out?

Does love burn out? Or is that a cop-out, an excuse to rationalize splitting up? Even the church seems to be buying the notion that if a relationship feels burned out, it is okay to drop it for the sake of individual fulfillment. Christians as well as non-Christians are accepting the idea that people are cheated and, therefore, justified in leaving if their partners fail to keep up or otherwise satisfy their desires.

Those who give up their relationships in favor of personal fulfillment lack a vision of what marriage can be—a vision that can motivate them to go back and look at what has gone wrong in the marriage and to make the necessary changes to bring real satisfaction.

Everybody admires the couple who have lived together fifty or sixty years and still care about each other and grow in their relationship. However, not everybody wants to put in the time and work required to achieve such a marriage.

All that we have when we die are the relationships we form with God and with others, and the things that have gone on in those relationships. If that's all we have in the end, shouldn't we be investing ourselves in bettering the quality of those relationships rather than stumbling over momentary discomforts and letting the relationships go?

Love Is a Talent

Even if our childhood experiences have not been overly harmful, none of us has developed a perfect ability to trust. We've all been loved imperfectly. As part of the legacy of sin, no relationship is perfect, and none of us is capable of perfectly receiving or giving love.

When I am working to help a couple overcome their mistrust and cultivate their love for each other, I often think of the Parable of the Talents (Matthew 25:14-30). In that parable, the servant was not condemned for possessing only one talent; rather, he was condemned for burying the one talent he had instead of investing and developing it.

So also, the husband or wife who possesses only one talent's worth of love, because of past experience, is not at fault. But he or she must surrender that *whole* talent to the other. It's not a question of how much is given, but of *how much of what one has* is given. When a husband or wife realizes that a mate is truly investing himself or herself to the limits of capacity, that goes a long way toward relieving superficial grievances. They are content to live with imperfection when they know a genuine intention is present.

When Christ died, He died to redeem us. He died to redeem all that was lost in the Fall, including—and perhaps primarily—our capacity for love. He bought back our ability to learn more and more how to love.

How do we learn? How is alienation undone in marriage? It is a circular process. We can't love until we have been loved. "We love because He first loved us" (1 John 4:19).

With Christ's love for us giving us strength and security, we need to take whatever talent of love we have been given and invest it, fully and freely, in our mate. We need both to listen and to talk, willing to set aside our own preconceptions, willing to stop hiding behind our own cultural mores, willing to be open and vulnerable to the other, and then to trust him or her to have the same intention.

We need to be willing to risk knowing and being known. As we grow in openness and understanding of each other, we grow in love. We overturn the obstacles that a sinful heritage and latent mistrust have placed in our way and, by God's grace, we draw closer to the ideal He intended for us.

If there is a problem, we need to say, "I want to know what I contribute to it, because I want to help change it." If both husband and wife can say that, there is always some way out. They may have to navigate through a swamp of misunderstandings and painful memories, but it is possible to arrive at solid ground. And when they do, their love will have grown so strong and deep that the relationship is virtually unshakable.

f o u r

Growing Away From Home

A licia was furious. Such a simple thing she had asked Jim to do, and now she'd have to do it herself. Their guests would be arriving before she had a chance to get dinner prepared.

They had had a long discussion and had agreed that since both of them had full-time jobs, it was only fair for both of them to attend to household chores. Jim had been the last to shower that morning, so Alicia had asked him to make sure the bathroom was clean and ready for company, and he had said he would. But here were towels hanging askew and water spots on the faucet and mirror. Wait until he got home—she'd give him a piece of her mind!

And she did, as soon as he walked in the door. Jim was taken aback at first, and then began the counterattack. He *had* cleaned the bathroom. Alicia was just too picky and obsessive about cleaning. Nobody was going to notice little water spots or care if all the towels were perfectly even and symmetrical. If this was the way she was going to act, she could just do all the cleaning herself. After all, he had almost missed his train by taking extra time to do the bathroom.

This may seem trivial, particularly to an outside observer. The incident, in itself, *is* trivial, as are thousands of other similarly minor transactions that take place in marriage. But though the incidents may be small, the issues underlying them are not: Both partners are negotiating how things will be done in the new family they are forming. In the process, they collide head-on with the necessity of breaking away, at an emotional level, from the families they grew up in. And that's not easy.

Alicia and Jim felt betrayed, wounded, and angry, as if the other had deliberately been hurtful; but the crux of the problem was their need to find a mutually agreeable definition of the word *clean.*

Alicia had been brought up by parents who were fastidious about their living space. Stray clutter and spots did not last long, or the person responsible for them was severely upbraided. Jim, however, had grown up in a more relaxed atmosphere that his parents described with comfortable pride as looking "lived in." His family wasn't sloppy, but they weren't meticulous, either. The house was given "a lick and a promise," and then the family was off on an outing, devoting most of their free time to having fun together.

So when Jim cleaned the bathroom, he got it looking pretty much as he remembered the bathroom back home looking before company came. But he judged himself finished with the task at about the point where Alicia's mother would have begun.

It took many conflicts over what "clean" was before Alicia and Jim began to listen to and understand each other's perspectives and to be ready to consider each other as allies with a common problem to resolve rather than as enemies to be subdued. As they worked on negotiating their differences in this area, they grew to realize that holding stubbornly to their parents' ways of doing things was not going to work. They both needed to give up a little of their own ideals and allow some of the other's style to form a new way of managing their own household.

In doing so, they knew they risked their families' disapproval. Alicia's mother never said anything outright, but Alicia knew the nonverbal signals that said her mother thought she had gotten a bit slack. And Jim got not only nonverbal signals but oblique comments about how his house sure looked nice, but his folks just couldn't seem to relax much while they were there.

Negotiations in marriage that involve breaking away from our families' "right way of doing things" are not easy. But they are absolutely necessary.

Honeymoon Suite for Six

When we think of the biblical safeguards around marriage, the prohibition against adultery is often what first comes to mind. As important as that is, though, it was not the first limit put on marriage. The first was: "Therefore shall a man leave his father and mother and shall cleave unto his wife, and they shall be one flesh" (Genesis 2:24, KJV). But leaving comes before cleaving. The health and vitality of the marriage bond requires that the first bond be left behind.

At first glance this seems a straightforward proposition. Naturally we leave home to get married. Why wouldn't we? Who would want to have their parents along on the honeymoon? Who, indeed! It happens more often than you might think—both figuratively and literally. It's as if six people are crowding into the honeymoon suite. But it's the two who just got married who feel the pinch.

I remember a couple who, after years of tension and low-grade fighting, finally came into marital therapy. Lois insisted that either they were going to get counseling or she was going to leave.

As they presented their situation, it emerged that never in their married life had they lived more than a block away from Jack's mother, Hilda. His father had died when Jack was a senior in college, and to comfort and care for his mother, he had gone home to live with her after graduation.

He had lived there many years before marrying Lois. In fact, their courtship and engagement had been prolonged for several years because it had never seemed to be quite the right time for him to move out of his mother's house. First she was recovering from surgery, then the roof needed to be repaired, then the basement flooded—Lois finally lost track of the reasons they were postponing their marriage. It was only when she began to talk about ending the relationship that a wedding date was set. (And then Jack's mother had come down with the flu the week before the wedding, throwing Jack into a panic of indecision!)

When Jack and Lois set up housekeeping in a nearby town convenient to Lois' workplace, Hilda started complaining about how hard it was to keep up her own big house. Would Jack look for a smaller place for her—perhaps in that cute little town he lived in now? It was just too hard to get out these days, or she'd look for a place herself.

None of the houses Jack found suited his mother until the one at the end of the block went up for sale. Hilda noticed it on a visit to Jack's home, arranged to see it the next day, and by the end of the week was signing papers and putting her own home on the market.

Thus began years of tug-of-war between Lois and Hilda, with Jack the increasingly frayed and bewildered rope. Whenever Jack was late getting home from work, or if he disappeared on a Saturday afternoon, Lois could invariably count on finding him at Hilda's house. When she complained about feeling neglected, Jack would nod as if he understood; but in actuality, her words were drowned out by his inner roar of guilty feelings and anxiety about abandoning his mother.

As before their marriage, it took the threat of Lois leaving to make Jack really pay attention to the problem. But even then, he had a hard time coming to terms with the changes he needed to make. He saw himself as having no choice about the way things were. Every time the couple tried to work out a viable solution to the problem, he would end up talking about what he "had to do" for his mother and how that prevented him from pleasing Lois. It was some time before he was able to accept the fact that Lois was to be the primary object of his loyalty, and that decisions he made needed to be based first on what his marriage needed, not his mother.

It took courage for Jack to risk hurting his mother by making decisions based on something other than her wishes, and he still struggles with all the feelings that this raises. But he truly loves Lois, and together they are working on making their marriage strong, and caring for Hilda within appropriate limits—which they, and not she, decide.

The Work of Adolescence

Disengaging from our parents, transferring family loyalties from them to our mate, is a lifelong process and can be a painful struggle. But it is also an exciting opportunity—an opportunity to redeem mistakes from the past and to combine the best from two families into a marvelous new creation, a family that has never been before.

Ideally, the process of leaving home begins before marriage, during adolescence. The teen years are notorious for the turmoil they bring to families, and with good reason. In reality, the whole family is disrupted and forced to change shape as the teenager struggles to become independent. Writer Phyllis Theroux recalls her own adolescence:

> *I was in [a] fog-bound bog of confusion. But I knew one thing: I hated my mother and could provide a long list of reasons why this hate was justified: She dressed funny, talked funny, even answered the phone funny. And the way she chewed her food was definitely not funny. I used to glare at her across the dinner table, as if the strength of my gaze could force her to alter the way her jaw moved. But it never did. She just kept on chewing in the same horribly annoying way.*

Her memory of herself as a teen enabled her to help a friend struggling to understand her own adolescent daughter's hostility. "In order for Ruthie to know who she is, she almost *has* to reject you. Otherwise, how else will she know what's you and what's her?"[5]

Teenagers must discover what they really think, feel, and believe, independent of what they have been told. In childhood they were guided by external incentives, rewards, and punishments. In adulthood, many of those external props will not be available; they will need a healthy stock of internal values by which to live. Adolescence is the time when they evaluate what they have been taught and then decide what they will keep and what they will change.

Stated that way, growing into adulthood sounds as if it were a fairly orderly, intellectual process. But if you remember your own teen years, you know that adolescence is like trying to keep your footing on a beach that is being battered by a stormy ocean. Even if you manage to stay upright, you can still feel the undertow sucking the sand from beneath your feet.

The very foundations of the young person's life are tested and challenged. Some will endure, others will not. The relationships that gave him those foundations will be strained and at times will seem to be disintegrating. But if those relationships have been healthy, they have tremendous potential not only to survive but also to be strengthened as they are redefined in terms of emerging adulthood.

The parents' role in all this is not easy. Indeed, it can be agonizing, for parents must risk letting go of their child if they wish the relationship to remain. The young person must really have the option of saying no to the parents and their values in order to be able truly to say yes. It is a bittersweet experience for both sides.

Hazards on the Way
All families struggle as they navigate a child's adolescence. Ups and downs and mistakes on both sides are inevitable.

However, some families make it especially difficult for a youngster to move away from them.

When parents have depended on their child for their own well-being, they will view his desire to separate from them as threatening. They may not consciously intend it, but in countless ways, verbal and nonverbal, they communicate that they cannot tolerate his moving away. He gets the message that if he is good, even though he may physically leave home, he will not leave emotionally by becoming different from them or by exchanging their values for others. In addition to the normal struggles of adolescence, he faces the threat that in becoming an adult he will lose his parents. If he lets them down, they may crumble.

Few teenagers can remain undaunted by that prospect. It is too high a price to pay, and so they will try to compromise by only seeming to become independent, while all the time never daring to consider who they really are, in and of themselves. They seem to live out their parents' values but never truly adopt those values as their own.

Another kind of family from which it is difficult to leave is the one that never formed a good parent-child bond. This lack creates problems for the adolescent striving toward adulthood. Not sure, at a deep emotional level, where he stands with his parents, the teenager may be reluctant to leave home, either literally or figuratively, until he feels on a solid footing with them. He waits for that original need to be filled in order to have the confidence to venture out on his own. Never having been fully able to trust his parents, he is unable to trust himself.

You Do Take It with You
There are varying degrees of ability to move toward independence, just as there are in bonding. So much depends on the strength of that parent-child relationship. In our imperfect world, we all grow up on one side or another of the ideal. And we carry both the healthy and the unhealthy aspects of our experience with us into marriage.

Now that may seem a risky way to enter married life. Why not work out all the bugs in the original bond first, before trying to form a new relationship?

Yet that is precisely where the challenge and excitement of marriage come in! Marriage is a new opportunity to become more of what we were meant to be, and our becoming is in the context of a loving relationship that has the potential of filling previously unmet needs in a way that will help us grow. In marriage—if we are willing—we become more aware of what we have brought with us from home, and grow in our ability to deal with it in an objective way. As we do so, we can make mature decisions about how we will let our background affect our present way of living. But what have we brought with us from home?

Great (and Not So Great) Expectations
Perhaps the most basic piece of "luggage" that we bring from home is the one that carries our expectations for marriage and our spouse. We have already looked at how our parents' expectations and their marital model may influence our choice of a mate. But that influence doesn't stop at the marriage altar. That's where it really begins!

As we grew up, we developed an eye-witness theory of marriage based on what we saw in our parents' marriage. In addition, we developed ideas of how married men and women should act, think, feel, communicate—in short, what we and our spouse should be like. Some of those conceptions were conscious and fairly concrete (e.g., a husband should be tall, dark, and handsome and should have a good job; a wife should be pretty, be an efficient homemaker, and love children). Many of our preconceptions, however, were unconscious. We may assume that our future spouse will be very much like our same-sexed parent. Or, if we were unhappy with that parent, we may, either deliberately or unconsciously, choose a spouse who is seemingly the opposite of that parent, and we will expect that he or she will not act or respond as that parent did.

In either case, however, we are not seeing our spouse for who he or she truly is, but are viewing him or her through the distorting lenses of our past experience. But because we are generally unaware of what we are doing, we assume our view is correct.

Sue grew up in an authoritarian home where Dad was a hardworking businessman, successful at what he did, and never lacking for a job. *His* father, though, had been out of work during the Depression, and the family had spent many anxious months trying to make ends meet. As a result, Sue's father had learned never to spend any more money than was absolutely necessary, and he demanded that his wife and children do the same.

So Sue was raised in a home that was financially secure, but where she had to justify every penny she spent, and where she often went without extras. By the time she was a teenager, she felt inferior to the other girls at school who seemed to have much nicer clothes, and she resented her father's control over her life.

She married Brian partly to be out from under the financial strictures she faced at home. Brian had freely bought her presents and taken her to nice restaurants while they were dating. While this was a delightful treat to her, it often gave her an oddly mixed feeling of guilt and triumph.

Though Sue was delighted with Brian's generosity, she assumed that all husbands and fathers had the same attitude about money. As soon as they were married, she unknowingly placed her image of her father over who Brian really was, and began to feel anxious every time she went shopping. If she ever bought anything for herself, which was seldom, she felt very guilty and would end up explaining to Brian at great length why she really needed the item.

She did not notice that Brian was not nearly as concerned as she was about how their money was spent. Because she mistakenly saw Brian as being like her father, she began to inwardly resent him for her anxiety and guilt. Fearing his rejection, though, she never told Brian about her feelings; instead, she let them pile up inside of her and became depressed.

For his part, although he was not overly concerned about spending money, Brian *did* expect that his home would always be immaculately kept and that meals would always be served at set times. His mother had been the epitome of the efficient, flawlessly organized homemaker and had gone out of her way to make sure that life at home always went smoothly for "her men." Brian assumed that marriage would mean a continuation of that style of life.

So when Sue, who was not particular about tidiness or time, failed to meet his expectations, Brian was hurt. He took Sue's casualness as an indication that she was not concerned about his needs. He expressed his hurt by becoming irritable and demanding, complaining whenever meals were off schedule or the house was dirty.

Needless to say, the glow soon wore off their marriage. Rather than growing closer together, they withdrew from each other. They did not understand why their marriage was more disappointing and frustrating than fulfilling, and each secretly blamed the other.

Unpacking the Baggage

Sue's and Brian's marriage was not hopeless. Nor is yours, even though you and your spouse may have the same kind of blind spots that Sue and Brian had.

Yes, we bring a lot of baggage with us to marriage. But it is important to unpack it, sort out the contents, and make competent decisions about what we will discard and what we will keep with us. And then, with our spouse, we can use what we have kept to forge a healthy, productive, functional new family. Marriage can be, in many ways, "the best of both worlds." How do we make this happen? Do we all need to see a marriage counselor to discover what is lurking beneath the surface?

Marital therapy has been, and continues to be, one course of action that many couples find very helpful in the unpacking process. But it is not the only one. Couples have within themselves God-given resources with which to help each other and their relationship. God has designed the marriage bond to be potentially therapeutic in itself. Besides fulfilling individual needs for comfort and closeness, it can also serve as a means to reach way back to the beginnings of those needs, to tap the root of who we are and what we carry with us from our families.

You may be like Sue or Brian—unconscious of the negative or unrealistically positive images with which you overlay your view of your spouse. You and your spouse may not be aware of exactly what you are doing; but your spouse will feel the effects of the image coming between you; and you will sense the intrusion when your spouse reacts to one of your in-laws rather than to the real you.

Growing away from home is a complex process that you and your mate are in together. You are the means God uses to help each other mature; and as you grow, your marriage grows, becoming more defined and beautiful.

It happens as you talk to each other, and as you listen carefully and caringly to each other. Together you can explore the families you came from, discovering what went into the people you are now. Can you share with your mate the joys and pains of your childhood? The hopes you had for exchanging hurts for healing? Or the dreams you cherished for finding someone as wonderful as Mom or Dad?

And can you listen as your partner tells you where he or she came from? Do you want to discover who he or she is now, as an individual, free from any overlay you might be tempted to impose?

Can you speak the truth in love to each other (Ephesians 4:15), communicating when you sense the intrusion of fantasy over reality? Can you be patient, kind, and firm in helping each other to let go of rose-colored illusions and to see your respective parents for who they are, good and bad together in their humanness?

Can you be there for each other, caring and supporting,

as you face disillusionment and accept the scars you have brought with you to marriage? And, having listened, can you see your partner for who he or she is, not demanding change to suit your fantasies but gladly accepting the gift of love offered you, however it is packaged?

As you do this kind of sharing with each other, something beautiful happens. You find yourselves gradually letting go of your parents' hands as you clasp each other's more firmly: A circular process is set in motion. The more you can accept your own families for who they are— strengths and weaknesses combined—the more you can accept each other as unique and precious individuals. As you do, and as your love grows on the solid base of reality, you are liberated to let your parents be who they are and to let them go. And in that letting go, you discover a new kind of love for them—the love of an equal for an equal, a love that forgives their failures and appreciates their gifts.

It is a natural process, yet it doesn't happen without work. Many times you will be called on to choose where your loyalties will be—back there or here with your spouse. And since the process is never perfect or complete, back there will sometimes seem safer than here. That is when the choice for here is painful. It is especially so if Father or Mother are reluctant to let go, and are tugging at your emotions. But the choice must be made. As in the spiritual realm, there can be no gain without loss.

Our Lord knew the necessity of being willing to let go of dependency on one bond in order to forge a new one. He said, "If anyone comes to Me and does not hate his father and mother, his wife and children, his brothers and sisters—yes, even his own life—he cannot be My disciple" (Luke 14:26). This use of the word *hate* was an emphatic way in the Hebrew culture of expressing a total detachment. Jesus knew we could not be rightly dependent on Him if we left the back door open as a way of escape into dependencies that might usurp His place in our lives.

In a similar way, though on a lesser scale, we must be

willing to "hate" our father and mother when we marry, forsake that dependency on our parents when it would continue to occupy a place that must now be filled by our husband or wife. It is forsaking, not rejecting; a leaving, not a casting away. But sometimes parents have difficulty perceiving it that way. Sometimes the adult son or daughter is faced with a situation in which it is necessary to say no to a parent in a way that seems unkind or is painful in order to grow in oneness with a spouse.

How does this square with the commandment to honor father and mother? (Exodus 20:12; Ephesians 6:2) It is as we are willing to see our parents for who they are, rather than for what we would like them to be, that we can truly honor them. As we dare to leave them, we communicate our respect for their separateness, our trust that they can deal with the pain of separation. And as we allow ourselves to become adult and rightly independent, we discover rich resources within ourselves that we may freely give back to them—not out of obligation but out of genuine love.

We may trust the wisdom with which God set up the family process. As we follow His prescriptions for family relationships, we participate in a process that generously provides for the needs of all involved. In letting go of our parents and clinging more and more closely to our mate, we create a marriage that will provide a rich and secure place in which our children may grow. Because we are sure of our loyalty to our marriage union, we reduce the chances that our children will be confused by the interference (either actual or figurative) of their grandparents. Instead, they will be able to benefit from the gifts given by our families, with no strings attached.

And we will be able to love our children rightly as they enter into their own marriages. Satisfied and unfettered in our own marriage, we will have the strength to keep our hands off as they begin unpacking *their* baggage.

f i v e

Portrait of a
Marriage

B arry and Janet have been married six years. Barry is a quiet man whose favorite pastime is reading about and collecting memorabilia from the American Civil War. He has become quite an expert on the subject and can talk about it at length when asked. In fact, his knowledge of the Civil War has gotten him through many otherwise strained moments in social gatherings; beyond commenting on the weather, he's not very good at small talk. Since childhood, Barry has preferred to observe people from a safe distance rather than be in the middle of a social interaction.

Janet, on the other hand, loves parties, committee and club meetings, and any other occasion involving a lot of people and action. She's usually at the center of whatever is going on. Besides being a witty conversationalist, she thrives on organizing activities and getting other people, including Barry, involved. Janet is the only reason Barry would even consider participating in their tenants' association.

Do Barry and Janet have a good marriage?

Bert and Lynn met in college, where he was the captain

of the football team and she was captain of the cheerleaders. Their on-again, off-again romance was a staple of the campus gossip mill, and there were bets on whether or not the two would actually get married. It was hard to tell which generated hotter sparks—their arguments or their reconciliations. Now, married ten years, Bert and Lynn are as competitive and as opinionated as ever, and are raising three scrappy athletes of their own. The noise level is the first thing noticed by new visitors to their home.

Charles and Ellen have all the accoutrements of family life in Suburbia, U.S.A. He's a bank executive who has made his way to the top by making smart decisions and by motivating his subordinates to do their jobs well. She's a devoted mother, PTA worker, Little League chauffeur, and husband-supporter.

Ed and Lois, on the other hand, are committed urbanites. Both are involved in demanding scientific professions and take overtime work as a matter of course. When problems or decisions come up in their marriage, Ed and Lois approach them the same way they approach an interesting research problem—considering all the angles and discussing possible outcomes and implications at length.

Which of these marriages are good? From the information I've given you about each one, it's impossible to tell. A good marriage is not identified by activities, noise levels, or patterns of dominance. Marriages, like people, come in all colors, shapes, and personality styles. It is the quality of the bond between the two partners, and what happens on the basis of that bond, that matters. Over the years I have come to recognize four elements that characterize healthy marriages: *empathy, valuing, loyalty* and *sexuality*. The presence and quality of these four factors determine the essential quality of the marriage.

Empathy

The American Heritage Dictionary defines *empathy* as "understanding so intimate that the feelings, thoughts, and motives of one are readily comprehended by another."

Another way of defining that understanding is "temporary identification." It is as if one, person duplicates inside himself the experience of another; and then, by identifying the feelings he experiences in that identification, he arrives at a conclusion about what the other's feelings must be. It is a process that takes far longer to describe than to occur. It happens in a split second, and we are usually aware of it only after the fact.

Watch the spectators at a gymnastics meet. While an athlete is involved in a difficult maneuver, you will see many of them biting their lips, grimacing, or clenching their fists. Written on their facial expressions and physical demeanor are the tension and striving of the athlete, though they may never have performed more than a somersault themselves. That's empathic understanding, arrived at through identification.

Most of those spectators will feel little concern for the athletes after the meet is over, but that makes no difference to empathy. It occurs just the same.

Falling in love is another story. There empathy takes place between two people who do have an interest in each other. When a man and woman begin caring for each other, it is because over the course of time spent together, they have come to identify with each other through a multitude of experiences, most of which have passed unnoticed. Shared struggles and triumphs have contributed to their bond, but so have dozens of supposedly insignificant daily events, from enjoying the surf together to digging her car out of the snow. One day they realize that they are in love with each other; but looking back, they would be hard-pressed to tell you exactly when their love began.

We practice empathy not only by identification with others' experiences but also through picking up their *affect*—outward signs of their inner emotional experiences. These are communicated, often involuntarily, through physiological changes.

Some cues we pick up are as obvious as a smile or a frown, but most are far more subtle—nearly imperceptible changes in the tension of the jaw, dilation of the pupils, flush of the skin, or stance of the body. We respond to those cues even when we are unaware of what we are responding to. Some people call this recognition *intuition* or *gut feeling* and want to dismiss it as unreliable. But it is real and valid and happens to everyone. Picking up signals from another's body language, we duplicate his feelings within ourselves, and we are with him emotionally even before we know what is happening.

It is this kind of empathy that enables a mother to understand her child. Even the newborn infant communicates his inner experience and feelings both vocally and through body language. His parent learns to read these signals and translate them into a meaningful interpretation of what the child might be experiencing. The child's affective cues become the parent's own awareness. Thus a mother will learn to interpret one kind of cry as "I'm hungry" and another as "I'm angry" or "I'm sleepy," based on the way she reads his affect.

As the infant develops physically and emotionally, the empathy becomes a two-way process as he learns to read his parents' facial expressions, tone of voice, and more subtle physiological signals. This can begin to happen as early as the child's first week of life, as soon as his eyes can fix on his parents.

The empathy that is experienced and learned in infancy and childhood becomes a part of the emotional equipment a person carries into adulthood. In marriage, the partners learn to read each other's affect and respond to each other on the basis of those readings. Each learns to feel with the other and arrive at an educated guess as to what he or she is experiencing. Many husbands and wives can tell from the sound of a footstep, the way the front door is closed, or how a coat is hung up (or not hung up) what kind of day a spouse had.

Unfortunately, many people stop at this point. As important as it is to be able to guess at and interpret another's feelings, this is only the first step in using empathy effectively.

The second step is to subject your guesses to the other's confirmation, correction, or denial. It is important to remember that until you have done this, your assumptions are just that—merely *your* assumptions. They cannot be treated as reality until the other person has said, "Yes, that's exactly how I feel." You owe it to him or her to check out whether your readings are accurate: "I'm getting the feeling that you don't like what I just said, am I right?" or "You seem a little 'down' today. Is anything wrong?"

Many marriages run into trouble at just this point. Stopping with the first stage of empathy, husband and wife begin to engage in a form of mind reading rather than true communication. The danger is that they base their readings and interpretations on what they have learned through their *own* past experience, especially their experience with their parents, rather than on the other's frame of reference. So, for example, a husband who often felt that he wasn't pleasing his parents might interpret his wife's frown to mean, "I'm unhappy with you," when she is actually thinking, "I'm really confused!" If he doesn't check out his assumption, he may react defensively and, before he knows it, be involved in an argument that neither of them wants.

To avoid this, he can take the time to give his wife feedback on the signal he is picking up and to tell her how he is interpreting that signal. "I see you frowning," he might say, "and I'm wondering if you disapprove of what I just did." When he does so, he will open the way for her to communicate what is actually going on inside her, and the two of them can talk realistically about what is happening between them. As they talk they will grow in their understanding of and caring for each other. In any relationship, but especially in marriage, this kind of communication is essential if empathy is to work constructively.

Valuing

Empathy is powerful. It can be used as a tool or a weapon. It can either build trust or instill fear, depending on how it is used. I can use my reading of another either to gain advantage over him or to discover how I might best help him or build a friendship with him.

Empathy occurs between all people, in every interaction between children and parents, between peers, between business associates. It even goes on between enemies; that's what defensive strategy is all about. Empathy does not require a positive relationship, and using empathy does not necessarily contribute to the growth of a relationship.

The presence of empathy alone, therefore, is not what distinguishes a good marriage. What matters is the kind of value that is placed on the feelings picked up through empathy. How important the other's experience is to me will determine what I do with my empathy and will either build or weaken the relationship.

What value do I place on my spouse? The answer to that question determines my ability to be truly devoted to my mate's interests. When I truly consider my spouse's feelings as important as my own, I will use empathy to support the relationship rather than wound it. It was this kind of valuing that the Apostle Paul was recommending when he wrote, "Do nothing out of selfish ambition or vain conceit, but in humility consider others better than yourselves. Each of you should look not only to your own interests, but also to the interests of others" (Philippians 2:3-4).

As I communicate my empathy in positive ways, demonstrating my care for my spouse and our relationship, I foster her trust. My spouse needs this and so do I. No matter how much in love I feel, I enter marriage with an inbred mistrust that will color my relationship with my mate. I am aware of areas in which I am vulnerable, and I can imagine all sorts of ways my partner could hurt me if parts of myself were known. Therefore it can be frightening to learn that she has insights into what is going on in me.

But if she respects me and, instead of crashing in with interpretations, handles my feelings with care and takes the time to check out assumptions, I can feel safe. I can be assured that what really matters is *my feelings,* not the other's achievement of insight. I can be confident that I can take the time to speak and be heard—even if I'm not yet sure what I am feeling. I have the freedom to explore what is going on inside me, knowing that it won't be grabbed away from me or used against me. I can trust that she won't trample on the things that are picked up from my involuntary body language but will wait until I can fill in with words what those signals mean. I won't be judged on the basis of her intuition; I will be allowed to explain myself. I can know that it is utterly safe to be myself, and this knowledge in turn breeds trust and freedom to share what's going on inside me.

Empathy is a skill that grows as it is used and as each partner takes the risk both of checking out assumptions and of letting the other in on what actually is going on inside. When a husband and wife use it in a way that treasures and cares for each other's personhood, it strengthens the bond between them as it clears up areas of misunderstanding and mistrust.

Loyalty

Close on the heels of how much I value my spouse is the question of loyalty. Where does she stand with me? How important is she in comparison to all the other people and circumstances—children, friends, hobbies, business—in my life?

In a healthy marriage, both husband and wife have an inner certainty that they are Number One with each other. But it's not a certainty that's necessarily settled once and for all. It comes up repeatedly for review and reconfirmation as new relationships and new circumstances enter the picture. A husband takes a new job with long hours. Is his wife still Number One with him? A new baby arrives. Is the husband's position with his wife still intact? An in-law comes to live with the family. Who will get priority?

We all have an urgent need to know that no matter what happens, we are our spouse's ultimate priority. So fundamental is this need that we cannot go long without testing the other's loyalty when we feel threatened. "I love you" and a peck on the cheek are not enough to still the fears of abandonment. Usually it takes a confrontation in which we can get our mistrust out. We may have to go through a painful experience of airing hurt feelings, doubts, and misunderstandings, and there is always the risk that in the end we will be misunderstood and rejected. But if a husband and wife really are Number One with each other, that knowledge will come through every time. Their bond grows as they continually reaffirm to each other, "Above all, I want *you*."

When conflicts and problems arise, there is no substitute for a husband and wife plumbing the question of their importance to each other. When one or the other is inclined to give their first allegiance to someone or something else, they need to go back and look at how important their spouse really is to them. When I am working with a couple who is struggling at this point, I often try to help them get to the bottom line by asking them to imagine what life would be like if they were to lose their husband or wife. The realization of how painful it would be to lose their spouse—and thus, how important that person really is to them—is often all it takes to help them order their priorities and reconfirm their loyalty to each other.

Sexuality
A lifelong marriage with sexual faithfulness to one spouse is the Christian norm, and for good reason. Sexuality flows naturally from the question of loyalty; the sexual relationship is the tangible statement that each is Number One with the other. And there can be *no other*.

When God instituted marriage, He instructed the husband and wife to cling to each other in preference to all other relationships. Our Lord upheld this principle in the strongest terms.

> *Some Pharisees came to Him to test Him. They asked, "Is it lawful for a man to divorce his wife for any and every reason?"*
>
> *"Haven't you read," He replied, "that at the beginning the Creator 'made them male and female,' and said, 'For this reason a man will leave his father and mother and be united to his wife, and the two will become one flesh'? So they are no longer two, but one. Therefore what God has joined together, let man not separate."*
>
> *"Why then," they asked, "did Moses command that a man give his wife a certificate of divorce and send her away?"*
>
> *Jesus replied, "Moses permitted you to divorce your wives because your hearts were hard. But it was not this way from the beginning. I tell you that anyone who divorces his wife, except for marital unfaithfulness, and marries another woman commits adultery" (Matthew 19:3-9).*

Marriage is a unique and exclusive relationship, and sexuality confirms its uniqueness and exclusiveness. The sexual relationship between a husband and wife was not designed just for physical release. It is part of the process of cementing the emotional and psychological bond between the two.

Historically, the church has seemed to set sexuality apart as a baser part of human experience. How misled! Sex is one of the most sensitive, tender ways a man and woman can experience intimacy with each other. It requires empathy, sensitivity to the other's desires and responses, a valuing of the other's feelings and experience, and an unwavering loyalty. Without these, it is not complete or satisfying. It falls short if it is merely one person cajoling or coercing the other into physical involvement. It can be truly satisfying only as each partner senses the pleasure and satisfaction of the other.

In the sexual act, empathy, valuing, and loyalty are confirmed and reconfirmed in ways that involve each partner's total being; there is no split between body, soul, and spirit. It is a person-to-person bonding.

A Portrait with Many Faces

What does a good marriage look like? How can it be described? It is one in which empathy, valuing, loyalty, and sexuality are ongoing, developing processes. Other elements are secondary: style of communication, activity, lifestyle, and dominance of one partner. Thus two marriages can be equally good but look entirely different from each other. So much depends on how the partners negotiate the differences growing out of their individual family backgrounds and their own bonding experiences.

Because of the uniqueness of each person's experience, every marriage will be unique in the ways husband and wife forge their bond with each other. One couple will be boisterous and even rough in their communication. Another will express their thoughts and feelings in well-modulated tones. One couple will thrive on activity while another will prefer quiet evenings at home. In some marriages, the husband will have the more dominant personality; in others, the wife will. All of these can be good marriages if they incorporate a growing empathy, valuing, loyalty, and sexuality.

The understanding between husband and wife is central to the process of building a good marriage, and it is a process that can be truly known only by those who are experiencing it. That is why, in the final analysis, no one can rightly judge another's marriage.

s i x

The Christian Marriage: In the Circle of God's Love

Years ago there was a Christian author who special-
ized in writing novels for young people. In those
books you could tell right away who was the Christian hero and who was the non-Christian bad guy. The
Christian was blond and clear-skinned; the non-Christian
was dark and had acne. So you knew from the outset who
was the winner and who was the loser.

It doesn't take much sophistication to know that color-
ing and complexion are the results of biology, not spirituality. Neither hair color nor skin tone has very much to do
with success or failure in life.

When it comes to describing relationships, however,
we're not always so sophisticated. To hear some Christians
tell it, Christian marriages are always beautiful and un-
blemished; only non-Christian marriages have scars. Likewise, Christian marriages always have a happy ending; non-
Christian relationships are doomed before they start.

Tell that to Henry and Sarah. Married forty-two years,
their continuing romance is the envy of many of their
friends and the aspiration of their grown children. The
medical practice that Henry retired from was highly suc-

cessful, and Henry's wise investment of his earnings has bought them a great enjoyment in their retirement years. They are fit and active and perhaps busier than they've ever been, dividing their time between visiting their happily married children, volunteering for charitable organizations, and serving on community boards. And their friendly, generous open-door style of hospitality makes them a favorite in the neighborhood. But there's no question that, busy as they are, their marriage is their primary pleasure and involvement.

The ideal Christian couple? They would shudder if you said so. They're agnostics. But healthy family backgrounds and personal strengths gave them a good start in a relationship which has developed a loving, lasting bond. Their marriage has not been problem-free, but it is certainly a far cry from the disaster some might predict for non-Christians.

Health is health, whether you're talking about skin or relationships. The One who "sends rain on the righteous and the unrighteous" (Matthew 5:45) designed marriage in such a way that, as it conforms to His original intentions, it will be loving and fruitful and a blessing to both spouses.

Does it really matter, then, whether a marriage is Christian? It certainly does! But I have felt it important, up to this point, to examine marriage as a human institution, rather than analyzing specifically Christian marriages. I believe there is a danger in starting off with an ideal of what is possible for the Christian marriage, without first understanding what marriage is in itself.

As a human relationship, marriage is a gift of common grace meant to serve a man and woman in their everyday lives. I do not want to set Christian marriage apart from what human life is really like. I don't want to give the impression that it is so unique as to be invincible—or virtually unachievable. It is important to understand what marriage was intended to be and *can* be as a human relationship before exploring the implications of making that marriage a Christian marriage.

Bonding with Christ

What makes a marriage Christian? Is it that husband and wife go to church together, pray together, read Scripture together? These acts do not, in themselves, make the marriage Christian. They may be evidences of spirituality, but they are not the substance. Marriage is not actualized by performance but by relationship.

In the last chapter we considered the qualities of empathy, valuing, loyalty, and sexuality as hallmarks of any healthy marriage, Christian or non-Christian. How are those qualities enhanced in a Christian marriage? What difference does it make that an individual or a couple is in touch with God—aware of His presence, resting on the availability of Himself and His resources, related and accountable to Him?

A common formula for Christian marriage describes the relationship between husband and wife as horizontal, and the couple's relationship to God as vertical, on a separate axis altogether. And of course the vertical relationship far outweighs the horizontal relationship in importance. The picture that emerges from this is that of a triangle, in which husband or wife can never be sure that they won't be set aside by the other in favor of a "higher calling." And they believe that they must be on guard lest they love their mate "too much."

Some of this thinking, I believe, comes from the way some have interpreted our Lord's words: "If anyone comes to me and does not hate his father and mother, his wife and children, his brothers and sisters—yes, even his own life—he cannot be my disciple" (Luke 14:26).

Was our Lord saying that He wants to *take the place* of husband or wife? That in belonging to Him, husband and wife cannot completely belong to each other? To say such a thing would be to fly in the face of what He intended marriage to be. I believe that He was making a distinction between His role and our spouses' roles, His place and their places in our lives.

Yes, our ultimate allegiance is to be to Christ, for He is Lord. Yet, paradoxically, our loyalty to Him frees us to give ourselves fully to our mates, making our marriage our primary human relationship. Our commitment to our mate must not violate our commitment to Christ; but at the same time, our commitment to Christ is not intended to violate our marriage commitment but to strengthen it. Christ doesn't compete; rather, He completes our marriages.

A relationship with Christ provides the context in which the empathy, valuing, loyalty, and sexuality of marriage take place. His completely trustworthy love provides the safety in which a husband and wife may learn, however stumblingly, to deepen their relationship with each other. They may falter but He will not. In Christ are the resources they need in order to continue working at giving themselves to each other. "His divine power has given us everything we need for life and godliness through our knowledge of Him who called us by His own glory and goodness" (2 Peter 1:3).

As they are surrounded by Christ's love, their relationship with Him is the reference point from which a husband and wife can look together at their marriage and find support for overcoming the obstacles that would stand in the way of their unity. Knowing that they have been forgiven by Him, they are free to take an honest look at themselves, let go of their defensiveness, and extend forgiveness to each other.

God is not an obstacle to the unity between a husband and wife; rather, He endorses their marriage. In Him, they find common values which provide a foundation for a marriage that will stand when other props—feelings, circumstances, or whatever else may have motivated their marriages—fail.

God does not intend for marriage to be a triangle in which the spouses can never be sure of their place with each other. He does not hover over our marriages, ready to jealously limit the love that flows between husband and wife. Christ dwells in the midst of our marriages, as He dwells in each Christian partner, and they live in Him. He is the vine; they are the branches (John 15:5).

Bonded to Him, as individuals and as a couple, they are free to grow in unity with each other and, together, with Him. Their love for each other is free to deepen simultaneously with their love and gratitude to Him for His work in their relationship.

Mistaken Identity

Let's look more closely at what it means to have Christ dwelling in us as individuals, and then in our marriages. A misunderstanding of spirituality has led some to believe they must somehow be other than human in order to glorify God. They misunderstand the admonition to live in the Spirit rather than according to "the flesh" (Romans 8:4-13) to mean that they are to annihilate their true selves and achieve some sort of mystical, otherworldly existence.

What they fail to grasp is that the Holy Spirit's function is to imbue their very humanness with His life and power. Not understanding that, they misguidedly try to adopt an identity shorn of as many human characteristics as possible. In doing so, they usually go one of two directions and become either Spiritual Superpeople or Submissive Concealers.

Spiritual Superpeople cultivate an aura of perfection. They are meticulous rule keepers; they are zealous church workers. They deny their inner emotional life and live on a plane that cannot be touched or understood by their "less spiritual" associates. Male Spiritual Superpeople often rise to positions of authority in the church and are revered from afar as they model the "perfect" Christian life and advise others how to live it.

Spiritual Superpeople often marry Submissive Concealers. The Submissive Concealer, usually a woman, looks at marriage as a sacrificial relationship in which her needs are always secondary to those of the Spiritual Superperson.

She finds it difficult if not impossible to say no to others' demands. Although sometimes aware of the pain this kind of existence brings, she presents a smiling face, accepting it as her lot to bear pain unflinchingly. As she locks her real self behind her polished exterior, avoiding any genuine disclosure of her hurt and anger, she isolates herself from meaningful relationships with her husband and children. Perceiving herself as powerless and insignificant, she falls back on covert ways of getting what she wants, sometimes through her children or through the church, and becomes "the power behind the throne."

Is this what it means to be spiritual? Does God intend for us to exchange our humanness for a spiritual persona in order to please Him?

Empty Vessels or Fulfilled Lives?

When the Apostle Paul wrote, "I have been crucified with Christ and I no longer live, but Christ lives in me" (Galatians 2:20), was he picturing himself as an empty vessel, someone from whom human personality had drained in order to make room for Christ?

I don't think so. Earlier in Galatians, Paul acknowledged being set apart by God from birth (1:15). God had a hand in who Paul was—his personality, family background, values, and all—from the beginning of his life. When Paul became a Christian, those things were not thrown out but redeemed and sanctified for God's use. His old orientation and enslavement to sin was replaced with a responsiveness to God and a capacity to live for Him (Romans 6:6-11; 8:2-9; Galatians 2:19). His perceptions and motivations changed, resulting in a change of behavior. But he still had the same body, the same nervous system, the same memories and experiences, the same basic personality characteristics he had always had.

Paul's identity was not obliterated but redeemed and renewed as the process of being conformed to the image of Christ was set in motion (Romans 8:29). He did not stop with writing, "I no longer live, but Christ lives in me." He went on to say, "The life *I live* in the body, *I live* by faith in the Son of God, who loved me and gave Himself for me" (Galatians 2:20).

Elsewhere Paul "boasted" of his humanity, knowing that God was glorified through his humanness and earthly circumstances (2 Corinthians 4:7-12; 12:7-10). God is glorified through "jars of clay" (2 Corinthians 4:7), humans living their lives *as humans.* When we become Christians, we do not become sanctified robots or dressed-up mannequins, but the persons we were created to be, increasingly able to reflect God's glory and image (2 Corinthians 3:18) and to enjoy the relationship with Him for which we were formed. God could not have fellowship with empty shells. He delights in relating to *people.*

Likewise, the marriage between a man and woman is not an empty vessel in the sense of being simply a receptacle to hold God. Marriage involves two humans who bring distinct personalities and experiences to their union, which itself develops a distinct personality. God dwells in the Christian marriage in the same way that He dwells in each Christian, bringing the marriage ever closer to the ideal He intended when He instituted it and using the unique characteristics of each marriage for His glory.

Unholy Triangles
Not understanding the place God wants in their marriages, some Christians attempt to triangulate with God, turning away from their marriages and putting Him between themselves and their mates. This can be acted out in a variety of ways, but whatever form it takes, it reflects an ambivalence about the marital relationship, a reluctance to fully trust and be committed to that union.

Those who triangulate this way often don't recognize that what they are doing says more about their feelings toward their mate than about their spirituality. If they acknowledge any distrust of the relationship or of their husband or wife, they identify it as justified distrust of their partner's spirituality and a reliance on the superior quality of their own commitment to the Lord.

• Triangulating with the church. The most common way Christians triangulate with God is by triangulating with the church, seeing it as an extension of God. Often it is a Spiritual Superperson who triangulates in this way.

Joan had married young, partly to escape an oppressive home life. Although she and her husband, Steve, had grown up in the same church and were Christians when they married, both saw marriage as a way to gain independence from their families and bypass restrictions they felt in their church. Soon after their marriage, they began to sleep in on Sunday mornings and became sporadic in their church attendance. When a job change led to a move to another state, they stopped going to church altogether and gradually let their Christian faith fade into the background.

But things were not running smoothly in their marriage. Three children and hundreds of arguments later, Joan was depressed and restless. Whatever unity she and Steve had once felt had dissolved. No longer did she look to him as an ally and companion or turn to him with her needs. She felt empty and desperately lonely.

One morning she happened to catch a Christian radio program and found herself feeling homesick for the faith she had left behind. In tears, she prayed that God would restore her.

Joan began attending church again and felt herself reunited in fellowship with God and His people. But then she began to look down on Steve as a backslider and urged him to get himself "right with the Lord" and come to church with her.

Steve was not interested. In fact, working six days a week, he resented Joan's repeated attempts to pull him from his Sunday morning sleep to go to church. What's more, he felt put down by Joan's insinuations that he was not measuring up as "spiritual head of the house," and grew more and more determined not to give in to her. He felt hurt and rejected and began resenting God for stealing his wife. He accused Joan of neglecting him and her responsibilities at home and tried to pressure her not to spend so much time at church.

But Joan was not dissuaded. The more the tension grew between herself and Steve, the more she clung to her new relationship with the church and her friends there. Already distant from Steve for years, she began to look to the pastor and other church friends to fill her needs, rather than struggling to work through the problems in her marriage. Her calendar filled up with Christian commitments—teaching Sunday School, helping with children's clubs, participating in an outreach program, attending mid-week prayer meeting, joining a Bible study, chairing the mother-daughter banquet committee, and generally being on hand whenever any church member had a need.

The pastor and church welcomed her with open arms, put her on a pedestal for her spirituality, and commiserated with her over her husband's waywardness. "Joan is wonderful," people would say. "So devoted to the work of the Lord. It's a shame she constantly has to fight against her husband dragging her down. We must uphold her in our prayers."

They did not understand that in "upholding" her, they were contributing to an undermining of her marriage, the relationship that God had intended, at a human level, to be her primary support and focus. Several years later, when Steve finally left home and filed for divorce, Joan's friends shook their heads and sighed over the hardness of his heart. No one, either before or after the divorce, helped Joan to see how she had contributed to the rift in her marriage. No one attended to her need to work at rebuilding that relationship.

Joan's situation is not unique. It can occur whenever one partner turns away from the other to have his or her needs met in a "more spiritual" way, even when both are members of the church. Marriages where only one partner is a church member are especially vulnerable, particularly when that one partner is married to a non-Christian. Pastors and church people, misguidedly heeding the call to be spiritual rescuers, rally around the churchgoer, little realizing that their real responsibility is to help that person by supporting his or her marriage, challenging him or her to work at building a union with his or her spouse. Scripture seems to teach that even when a believer is married to an unbeliever, that marriage is meant to stand and can be a vehicle of God's grace (1 Corinthians 7:12-14, 16).

• Triangulating with a Christian vocation. Closely akin to triangulating with the church is the tendency of some Christians—also often Spiritual Superpeople—to give their attention, energy, and loyalty to Christian service, whether as professionals or laymen. Because Christian service is commendable and is endorsed both by Scripture and by the Christian community, it is easy to miss the fact that such service may sometimes be motivated more by difficulties in a marriage than by commitment to a calling. When a husband spends long hours working overtime for a corporation, it is easy to point out the ways he is shortchanging his ·marriage. But when he instead devotes those long hours to ministry, one almost feels guilty calling his attention to the needs at home.

The Apostle Paul rightly observed that Christians who are married have a dual calling: to serve the Lord and to serve their spouses. They are not free to give themselves one hundred percent to a Christian vocation at the expense of their marriages. To those who believe they should give themselves totally to the Lord's work, he gave the advice to remain unmarried (1 Corinthians 7:32-35).

• Triangulating through prayer. Sometimes, instead of confronting each other and working through problems in the relationship, one or the other of the partners—the Submissive Concealer—will adopt a policy of taking marital difficulties only to the Lord in prayer, without presenting the problems to the spouse. "I'm just trusting the Lord to work things out," that one will say. "After all, He's all I need; He's the only one I should really trust."

At the risk of sounding unspiritual, I'd like to challenge that practice. Certainly I believe in prayer and in the need to commit all our concerns to the Lord. But I also believe that if the one praying about her partner really listens to the Lord's answer, she is likely to hear, "If your brother [or husband or wife] sins against you, go and show him his fault" (Matthew 18:15; cf. Leviticus 19:17; Luke 17:3). "If you are offering your gift at the altar and there remember that your brother [or husband or wife] has something against you, leave your gift there in front of the altar. First go and be reconciled to your brother [or husband or wife]; then come and offer your gift" (Matthew 5:23-24).

God intends that we work through differences *in* the relationship. Yes, God wants to hear our concerns about our marriages, but not as a substitute for evading what is necessary to work through alienation or mistrust that exists between us and our spouse. He doesn't want to be privy to our secret complaints that we are not willing to bring up with our mate. God doesn't take sides, much as we might like Him to. The fact that we are praying about our mate doesn't assure our spiritual superiority or enlist the Lord's favor for our position. He deals not in competition but in reconciliation. He will not support one partner at the expense of the other. His interest is that the two work together to uncover the source of the problems and to build a firmer bond.

Putting It Together

So how *are* we to build a Christian marriage that honors the Lord without becoming a triangle?

First, remember that marriage was made for all humans, even those who don't know the Lord. The principles that apply to any marriage apply to the Christian marriage. To the extent that marriage brings good to both husband and wife, it honors the One who designed it. We must work on building the empathy, valuing, loyalty, and sexuality that give health to any marriage. And what better foundation to build on than Christ Himself. In Him husband and wife find a basis of trust, a value that goes even deeper than the marriage relationship. That relationship to God—more important than but not competitive with their marriage—gives the two of them a point of reference from which to work on their marriage.

This is especially important in times of conflict. Rather than drawing away from each other and judging each other's spirituality, the Christian husband and wife can go back to acknowledging the bond they have in Christ. If I am open to considering my Christian partner's love for God as being as deep as my own, and his or her concern for godly living as strong as my own, then we have a basis of trust from which to work on our problems.

I must be willing to suspend my judgment of my partner's spirituality, and my satisfaction with my own, long enough to listen and to hear what is going on with him or her. So much of what we label spirituality is in reality an overlay derived from our culture, our family's way of doing things, or our own defensive coping. Am I willing to come out from behind that and be real, and let my partner be real, so that together, before the Lord, we can root out the alienation?

Two people do not have to have identical perceptions of who God is in order to have a good marriage. In fact, they *can't*. So much of the way we see God depends on our individual past experience with nurturing and with authority, which shapes our expectations of who He is. If I can respect the fact that my partner's background leads to different perceptions of God—and that those perceptions may be just as valid as my own—I can respect and trust his or her relationship with Christ. We can talk about, empathize with, and learn from the differences and at the same time discover and affirm the points where we agree. This is a very important means God gives us to come to a more complete understanding of who He is—perhaps even more important than what we learn from the pulpit. Our differences do not have to divide us; our common relationship with Christ is more important than those differences.

In the final analysis, relationships are based on values, not just feelings. It is what is important to the two of us that gives a foundation to our marriage—what we trust and live by and would die for, if necessary. When the two of us share a loyalty to Christ, we are free to commit ourselves to a trusting relationship in which we can be confident of our worth to each other. The knowledge that we are of value—something we should begin to learn in childhood—is to be confirmed and demonstrated in marriage.

A trust in each other's good faith is basic. If that is not present, we must go back and look at what *was* there that drew us together. And we must not approach that question with a good guy/bad guy mentality. Marriage is a joint responsibility, as are problems in the marriage. I cannot complain about my "less spiritual" partner; I *chose* that partner. I have no right to look *outside* the marriage for what God ordained to be provided *by* the marriage. If there is mistrust between us, it must be flushed out and looked at, talked about and resolved. There is no other recourse. And it is work we both must do. Christ doesn't magically make our marriages better without our own participation in the process.

In some marriages one of the partners may come to know Christ even though the other partner does not. That is a difficult situation, but the Christian partner dare not consider himself or herself superior because of that relationship with the Lord. He or she must still value the other deeply and be utterly loyal, whether or not the other turns to Christ. Such a stance requires being able simultaneously to want the other to be a Christian and yet allow him or her not to be. (And after all, isn't that what God does with all of us?)

To turn away from the non-Christian partner toward God or the church damages the relationship and ultimately works against God's glory in the situation. The non-Christian partner will receive the mistaken impression that God is a rival who wants to take his or her partner away, rather than One who is eager to pour out His blessings on the marriage and give the two partners more completely to each other.

The Circle of God's Love

What is a Christian marriage? Not a triangle but a circle. God's love is the unshakable pivot around which husband and wife can safely entrust themselves to each other and the circumference within which they can live and grow in increasing unity. When their relationship with God is central and all-encompassing, they are free to welcome each other as the Number One person in their lives, knowing that their relationship ultimately depends not on each other but on God Himself. It is His loving gift to each of them. Their commitment to each other is anchored by their commitment to Him. They give themselves to each other in the light of His presence, blessing, and judgment.

part 2

MAKING THE MARRIAGE
WORK

Secrets

I said I need you to pick up some things at the store on your way home from work."

"What? Oh, sure, no problem. What do you need?"

Sara sighed. "Honey, what's wrong? You've been walking around in a fog for weeks now. Is something on your mind? I feel as if I'm living with a stranger."

"Hey, I'm just tired. No problem. Just a lot of pressure at work. You know. No big deal."

Well, maybe it was no big deal to him, but Sara was getting tired of feeling as if Joe were on another planet, even when he was in the same room with her. Besides, she didn't believe him. He'd been under pressure at work before, but in all the ten years they had been married, she had never felt him so distant. Something *was* on his mind, and he wasn't telling her. But what could she do? He obviously wasn't going to give her a straight answer.

Frustration and fear vied within her as she pondered this suddenly foreign husband of hers. His cheery good-bye as he left for work served only to unsettle her further.

There was something between them. And it was a secret.

The Meaning of Secrets

"I know something you don't know!"

How often when we were children did those words, flung at us in smug singsong, cut deep into us, making us feel shut out, somehow inferior?

But if a friend says, "I want to tell you something I've never told anyone before," we are instantly drawn in. We feel special, trusted, an honored part of an exclusive relationship.

We all have private parts of ourselves—feelings, memories, experiences—that we protect and care for as we would a vulnerable child. We all have sacred territory that we guard—and rightly—against careless trespassers. Secrets are a part of our individuality.

Sharing a secret is no light matter, for a secret told is an entrée to the inner life, the soul. How you parcel out those secrets—those things that are personal, that bear special emotional significance, that reveal special hurts or joys, special weaknesses or growth—reflects how you value the person to whom they are given. They show how much you want the other to be part of yourself, to be able to influence, criticize, and support you.

In the process of marital bonding, a man and woman becoming one, the management of secrets plays a key role. Choosing to keep or tell a secret either limits the bonding or furthers it. As a consequence, I have come to regard secrets as a sort of barometer in a marriage. When a husband and wife keep large areas of their lives hidden from each other, that tells me something about their level of bonding. When it is evident that they have been allowing each other to participate in some of the inner processes of their lives, I know that the bonding is well underway.

Bonding is a process that takes the lifetime of a marriage. While the road to oneness can be a joyful journey, it is not without its terrors. No less than one's very self is at stake; one's whole being is offered for potential rejection. Yet there is no other way to find true acceptance. The extent to which one locks away secret areas of his or her self from a marriage partner is the extent to which one still does not feel that self to be accepted. There is no security without risk.

Sharing Secrets in Courtship
The hazards of telling secrets are great, and few relationships are safe enough to contain them. But marriage is one relationship that not only is designed to carry the weight of our secrets but *must* carry them.

However, we don't wake up the day after our wedding instantly ready to divulge all to our mate. Sharing must begin in courtship. That is where the first testing of intimacy, the first sharing of secrets, occurs. Courtship is a transitional, uncertain time. The unknowns of a future sexual relationship are by no means the most sensitive or frightening aspects of growing toward marriage. Far more intimidating are the prospects of letting someone else in on those secrets that make us who we are. Yet scary as it is, we find ourselves more or less irresistibly drawn into the dangers of self-disclosure.

Throughout adolescence we worked on separating from our families, beginning to keep secrets from them as we forged an identity distinct from our parents.

What we find in early adulthood, though, is that we begin bursting with those secrets, aching to have someone with whom to share them, someone to whom we can reveal who we are.

Courtship offers the first opportunity to begin to form the intimacy we crave. At least, it could. Unfortunately, in our culture courtship often becomes instead a reinforcing of secrets, a feat of salesmanship, an attempt to convince the other of our flawlessness. He hides his vulnerability to hurt. She carefully sidesteps issues that make her feel inadequate. They both fear that if weaknesses and needs are exposed, the relationship will crumble and they will be alone again.

As a preparation for problem-solving and mutual meeting of needs in marriage, the premarital period *must* include the disclosure of who we really are. We must let ourselves be known as imperfect people who need each other. It is during this time that we start to test the other's acceptance of us and response to our weaknesses. This is when we begin weaving the fabric of trust and permanence that will be able to withstand the exposure of our secrets.

Some of the secrets that need to be told during courtship are the ones that have to do with family backgrounds. If they aren't shared, they inevitably sneak out later, sometimes with disastrous results.

What other secrets need to come out during courtship? Should you, for example, tell your fiancé about previous sexual experiences? Let's ask it another way. If asked directly about past sexual experience, would you be comfortable with telling the truth, or would a lie be a tempting alternative?

Lies are death to a relationship. For one thing, they never exist in isolation, but require more lies to support them. And one lie left unconfessed or unchallenged gives permission for all that follow. No lie is ever perfectly kept in a close relationship. It opens a fissure which, no matter how narrow, will be deep enough to cause feelings of separation.

The degree to which previous relationships are a problem to the one involved is the degree to which they will be a problem later in the marriage.

Amy and Jeff ran into serious problems on this point. When they entered marriage, Amy was a virgin and believed Jeff was also, although she had never directly asked him. But several years earlier, before Jeff was a Christian, he had been involved in a year-long sexual relationship. When he became a Christian, he broke off the relationship and considered it a closed chapter in his life. During his engagement, he sometimes wondered whether he ought to tell Amy about that relationship, but fear held him back. He knew that she held strong Christian convictions and had never been involved sexually with any man, and he imagined that she would be appalled and disgusted if she knew about his past sexual involvement.

So he opted not to tell her. After all, he reasoned, that relationship ended long ago, the woman no longer meant anything to him, and he saw no reason for creating a problem.

But the fear and sense of guilt that kept Jeff quiet, rather than fading away, grew as the months passed. Every time he made love to Amy, he would subconsciously wonder whether she would still love and respond to him if she knew about his past. Though he couldn't put it into words, he began to have a sense that he was cheating her, that her love was something he had obtained by fraud. The more his guilty anxiety grew, the more he felt resentful and unworthy of her.

Needless to say, their sexual life suffered. Although Jeff was still able, at first, to share with Amy in other areas of their lives, he began to withdraw sexually in an unconscious attempt to quell his anxiety and lessen his guilt.

Of course, Amy knew nothing of all this, but she saw that Jeff was becoming more and more remote. She alternated between doubting her sexual attractiveness and being angry at what she perceived as his rejection of her. She never asked him about what was going on, lest her worst fears be confirmed; but the hurt that was mounting in her found expression in anger, sarcasm, and attempts to hurt him.

Already feeling inferior to her, Jeff responded with putdowns of his own. By the end of their first year of marriage there was barely any personal communication between the two that was not tinged with resentment, and both began to wish they were free of the marriage.

Fortunately, an alert friend, who knew how happy they had been during their courtship and was puzzled by the rapid deterioration of the marriage, had the courage to suggest they talk to a counselor. Not really wanting a divorce, in spite of the animosity they felt toward each other, they decided to give marriage counseling a try.

The counselor met with them together at first, and then had an individual session with each of them. It was during Jeff's individual session that the old secret finally came out. The counselor immediately perceived a connection between the guilty secret and the couple's present distress, but he had a hard time convincing Jeff of it.

Even after he could acknowledge the effect the secret was having, Jeff was reluctant to share it with Amy, fearing it would be the death blow to their already badly wounded relationship. But he finally realized that although sharing the secret would be risky, not sharing it would only perpetuate and aggravate their problems.

The session in which he finally told his secret was excruciating. Difficult as the secret was for him to tell, it was even more difficult for Amy to hear, and at first it only seemed to increase her feelings of anger and betrayal. Her reaction was so strong that even their counselor wondered whether it had been wise, after all, to let the secret out.

But it proved to be the turning point in their relationship. After the initial shock, both Jeff and Amy rallied and began to work purposefully on their marriage. Now they both knew the roots of the bitter feelings that had grown up between them. Sorting through them all, they deepened their understanding of themselves and each other and eventually were able to offer and receive true forgiveness for real and imagined wrongs.

I would in no way endorse a confessional in which one searches one's soul and reveals every sin ever committed. But a need to hide one's history poses a potential for problems later. The need to hide says, "I'm not ready to trust. I don't believe that your acceptance of me is genuine and complete. I feel safer if you have illusions about me rather than the truth. I expect that truth will bring disillusionment and rejection."

The things that are known and worked through by a

husband and wife give strength to the relationship. But whatever remains secret is like a hidden cavity that threatens the structural soundness of the marriage.

Sharing Secrets in Marriage
If sharing secrets in courtship is important, how much more important it is to share them in marriage. A secret is anything that is emotionally significant to both husband and wife but which is hidden by one from the other. What gives a secret its significance is not so much the content as the meaning of the content. A secret can be as seemingly innocent as planning for a vacation or a job change without letting the other know, or as obviously harmful as an affair. Withholding information is only the surface of a secret; its essence lies in what it means to the marriage.

Some secrets are *family* secrets. A father abandons his family, and only a few people inside the family know why. A sister lives for a while in another state "for health reasons" and returns with a weary sadness that no one talks about. A mother's alcoholism is euphemised as being "under the weather"; a brother's gambling debts are carefully covered by a doting parent's bank account. Dutiful family members are expected to keep these secrets.

But the fact is that families *don't* keep secrets very well. Sooner or later, a well-meaning or malicious relative will let slip to a husband or wife a secret about the mate's background. The effect can be devastating. Mistrust springs up like a weed and both husband and wife become hurt and defensive. "Why didn't you tell me this before?" or "You never did like my family!"

Letting a family secret remain between spouses is never wise, but it can be so tempting. Sometimes a fear of parental rejection keeps the secret intact; sometimes a misguided sense of obligation. But letting a spouse in on family secrets is a necessary part of the process of choosing loyalties, leaving the old family in order to form the new one, whatever the risks. Family secrets are a part of who we are. A marriage partner needs to know them.

Sometimes partners keep secrets from each other about *finances*. A husband earns a little extra on the side and spends it without letting his wife know. A wife borrows from the grocery fund to buy an expensive dress which she tells her husband was on sale. One partner makes a major purchase that wasn't discussed or planned by the two together and which goes beyond their budget. One partner (often the husband) has complete jurisdiction over the bookkeeping and the other never has a clear idea what their actual financial status is, let alone how to manage such things as insurance and mortgage payments.

Certainly a husband and wife should have a measure of freedom in earning and spending. They should have equal access to the family finances. But how much can one spend before it is perceived by the other as taking away from the family? Significant spending that is not discussed and agreed upon by both partners is a sign of division between them. Secrets about money, and the mistrust, accusations, denials, and lies that go with them, grow between the two and split them apart.

Sometimes *a third party*—a friend of the same or opposite sex—becomes a secret. A husband or wife, without the knowledge or permission of the spouse, talks to this sympathetic friend about the marriage. Such a practice is devastating because it says that that friend is more trustworthy than the spouse. It essentially makes that friendship more important than the marriage.

When the friend is someone of the opposite sex, the stage is set for an affair, which by its very nature is a powerfully destructive secret. The affair strikes so profoundly at the heart of what marriage is all about that not to confess it is to admit that the marriage no longer has a place of priority. The revelation of an affair can be a shattering experience. I would never minimize that. Yet untold, it will erode the marriage from underneath until there is no means of restoration. Told, it can provide the opportunity for forgiveness. The forgiveness must be profound, dealing with all of the messiness of the wound, not just covering it over.

At the most basic level, our secrets involve not just situations and experiences but the thoughts and feelings that surround those experiences and make us who we are.

Sometimes our secrets are so well hidden that even we have forgotten their existence—until our partner tugs at a locked door and inquires what is behind it. A spouse may probe at an area that reawakens forgotten pain, or may sense and comment on a feeling that is stirring inside of us that we had until then been able to deny.

In a social relationship, such poking and prying might be considered rude and intrusive, but in marriage it is absolutely necessary. Not only do marriage partners need to be known, but also they need to know as much as they can about each other, in order for each to incorporate the other in their lives. They have a right to pry.

When secrets are kept, they divide. When they are shared, they forge another link in the bond between husband and wife.

Why Do We Keep Secrets?
We all have a sense of the power and importance of secrets. We have all experienced the distance when secrets are kept, the closeness when they are divulged.

So why do we keep them? Are we so bent on evil that deception is our primary goal? Not necessarily. Sometimes our keeping of secrets is a matter of being too busy. We don't consciously intend to keep the secrets, but we just don't take the time to talk.

Innocent as that may seem, there is usually a reason for not talking that goes beyond the amount of time available. Why don't we take—or make—the time to share with our mate? If we postpone saying something, there is a reason. Very often the reason lies more with our hesitations about intimacy than with the clock.

We withhold secrets in direct proportion to our suspiciousness or our need to be alone. Keeping a secret may not be simply an indication that we do not value our partner. It may be more a reflection of how we feel about being connected with *anyone*. Perhaps we learned very young that we were expected to manage the tough times in life on our own. No one wanted to hear our private hurts and fears. Or perhaps we were hurt or betrayed by a confidant and learned to fear sharing. Experiences like those taught us to be wary of revealing too much.

Guilt, insecurity, and fear are often at the root of a secret. We carry a guilt that we doubt will be forgiven. We expect rejection rather than acceptance. We fear being misunderstood, blamed, forever looked upon with disgust or contempt. We expect that a secret divulged will label us for life, be held over our heads and used against us.

Such fears often have their roots in childhood. They are part of the baggage we bring with us to marriage. When a person grows up experiencing disgrace but not forgiveness for misbehavior, an almost indelible mark is left on the soul. The child whose misbehavior is thrown again and again in his face will have little reason to believe that the telling of a secret can bring anything but repeated humiliation.

Marriage offers no magical cure for mistrust bred since childhood. We expect in marriage that which we experienced back home. But marriage *can* be the beginning of learning something different. A creative, redemptive emotional experience is one in which one begins to prove that a spouse can be trusted in areas where others could not.

Sharing Secrets: Intimacy Versus Dependency

Sharing is a two-way street. In developing intimacy it is not enough to spill out whatever comes to mind. You must also work to establish the kind of climate in which your spouse can also let go of secrets. You must regard your partners' secrets as equal in value and sensitivity to your own. Sharing means not only revealing your secrets but also receiving your mate's.

Paradoxically, sharing too much too soon can be just as harmful to a relationship as withholding secrets. Rather than contributing to true closeness, such sharing sets up a dependent, symbiotic relationship in which one party seeks to have his or her identity absorbed by the other. Perhaps you learned that you *had* to have someone supporting you at all times, and you never learned that you could have your own secrets and be properly independent. Carrying such a belief into a marriage will not foster intimacy but prevent it. True intimacy occurs between equals, both individuals in their own right.

Sharing too little or too much—either way there are dangers. Usually, however, we err on the side of sharing too little, protecting ourselves too much.

Must We Tell All?

A secret forms a weak place in a marriage. Must we therefore tell all? Must every detail of past history and present experience be laid out on the table?

Obviously that would be both impossible and impractical. There aren't enough hours in the day to cover every aspect of our experience, even if we were able to keep up a running commentary. So naturally there will always be things left unsaid.

The key question is, "Why the secret?" Remember, a secret is something untold that bears emotional significance to the *two* partners. Thus, for example, going out for lunch may or may not be a secret. It is a secret if you feel a need to hide it—because you ate in an extravagantly expensive restaurant when your budget was already strained, or because you went with a secret friend, or because it was the occasion of transacting some business you didn't want your mate to know about.

A rule of thumb is: "If you are asked, can you tell?" And you may well be asked—particularly about those things you are tempted to keep hidden. Secrets have a way of hanging in the air and making their presence known. They are picked up and felt by a spouse even when there is nothing obviously tangible to go on. Averting the gaze, a studied casualness when a certain subject is brought up, an almost imperceptible stiffening of the muscles, a laugh that is too hearty—we give ourselves away in dozens of ways. Those nonverbal messages, unless they are addressed and explored, become a framework for mistrust, doubt, questions. A secret is often felt before it is known, and its unseen presence will gnaw at the relationship until it is revealed and dealt with.

But what about protecting one's spouse from the effects of a secret? "It would just hurt my loved one's feelings," we rationalize. Or, "I shouldn't bring up such a petty issue; I just need to clear up my own attitude."

Yes, sometimes it is appropriate to postpone telling a secret. Sometimes the other person is not ready or in a position to hear, digest, and benefit from what a mate wants to share.

For example, a wife may see her husband meting out what she believes to be overly harsh discipline on the children. She also knows that he has been under an unusual amount of job stress recently and is struggling to feel competent in many areas. To come in swinging with denunciations of his parenting will be experienced as a threat, a put-down.

By waiting for a time when he is feeling more relaxed and more sure of himself in other areas of his life, and then broaching the subject in such a way that she communicates also her respect for his intentions to be a good father, she not only gains a hearing for her own thoughts and feelings but also opens the door for him to explore the meaning of his behavior. Perhaps his own father was demanding in the same areas in which he is putting pressure on his children. Maybe his insecurities about himself make him anxious about the children's performance. Sensitive timing in letting a spouse know what we are experiencing encourages rather than shuts down the free exchange of secrets.

Sometimes you may not be sure of all your own thoughts and feelings about a matter. You need time to sort them out and gain more understanding of yourself before speaking. That too is legitimate.

But be sure your withholding of information is born of genuine wisdom, not a fear of dealing with the issue or a mistrust of your partner's ability to handle it. Are you temporarily or indefinitely postponing the subject? Are your intentions to avoid or to facilitate dealing with it? Are you waiting until you have done some necessary working through of the issues, sorting out your feelings and formulating your thoughts? Or are you swallowing your feelings, trying to deal with a relational issue on your own rather than with your partner?

By their very nature, some secrets destroy—sexual secrets, the affair, the outright lie. Whatever pain they may cause the spouse, they have to come out. Both partners must submit to the pain of surgery or they will suffer the ravages of a cancerous secret. There is no hope for health in a relationship that harbors these secrets.

Can You Keep a Secret?

"There is nothing concealed that will not be disclosed, or hidden that will not be made known," said our Lord (Matthew 10:26). Any keeping of secrets in marriage is a temporary game. Ultimately all will be known; ultimately there will be no secrets. "Whatever is has already been, and what will be has been before; and God will call the past to account" (Ecclesiastes 3:15).

The God who yearns for relationship is the God who has spent the whole of history and eternity progressively revealing His secrets, insistently disclosing to us the knowledge of who He is and His purposes in the world (Romans 16:25-26; Ephesians 1:9-10; 3:3-12; Revelation 10:7).

The process of bonding between husband and wife, as they let each other in on their secrets, is a participation in the very nature and purposes of God. In a future day we shall know even as we are known by God (1 Corinthians 13:12). In this life we can begin to experience the freedom of stepping out from behind our secrets as we enter into relationships with others and particularly with our mate. In marriage we have opportunity, as in no other relationship, to begin revealing the mystery of who we are.

The Problem of Power

Jack and Liz were at it again. The subject matter was different from the last quarrel, but the theme was the same: who was going to have the upper hand?

As I listened to this latest battle in their ongoing war, I heard not two selfish people lusting for power but two scared people who were afraid of letting go and entering into an intimate relationship with each other.

My emphasis in this book is *the intimate relationship between two people, the oneness that grows in a marriage when husband and wife open up to each other, let each other know who they are, allow each other to come into areas of their lives where no one else has been before.*

Power protects and defends itself against the other person. Intimacy opens itself up.

Power says, "Because I feel inadequate, I'm going to work hard to hide my vulnerability and need; I'm going to beat you down before you beat me down." Intimacy says, "Because I know I am incomplete on my own, I want you to be part of me."

Power trusts only its own control over another. Intimacy ventures into an ever more trusting relationship.

Power frustrates intimacy. Intimacy takes away the need to wield power.

When a couple is primarily concerned about who is going to have control in their marriage, intimacy is not working for them. Something has gone wrong in their mutual trust, caring, openness, and refusal to have secrets, and unquestioned loyalty to each other. Failing to achieve intimacy, they have taken a fall-back position in which each one strives to maintain power or rights or territory.

In one sense, power is the ability to perform a function or to cause an effect. But when it is taken to mean one person exercising control over another—and at the expense of the other—power becomes a negative. Such power plays work against a relationship. Marriage was designed as a refuge where a man and a woman could meet each other's needs, not as an arena for power struggles.

Where the Struggle Began

Before the Fall, the selfish use of power was not an issue in marriage. Adam needed someone with whom he could relate at the deepest level, someone with whom he could share every aspect of his being. And so the Lord created Eve, much like him but separate from him, someone designed to be one with him. She was exquisitely suited to his needs, as he was to hers. Neither had any thought of lording it over the other or using the relationship to selfish ends. Each was devoted to the good of the other and of the relationship, and both were devoted to God. They lived together in harmony, intuitively meeting each other's needs and enjoying unity in their tending of the Garden.

Then sin entered, and with it a rift in the relationship. Self-interest took first place, ahead of their concerns about their relationship (Genesis 3:12-13). Self-interest is the stuff of which power struggles are made. It is no accident that almost immediately after the entrance of sin into the world, marriage was given a structure, with the husband ruling over the wife (Genesis 3:16). In their now fallen state, mutuality and unbroken consensus could no longer be taken for granted. There had to be some recourse when intimacy and mutual concern failed.

That is not the whole story, though. To take the Genesis passage alone as the blueprint for marriage is inadequate. The whole of Scripture is the story of God's redemptive activity to restore the design He had originally intended for individuals and families. Paul's description of the Christian marriage is a hymn of triumph affirming that we may aim for the oneness God intended for marriage.

Submit to one another out of reverence for Christ. Wives, submit to your husbands as to the Lord. For the husband is the head of the wife as Christ is the head of the church, His body, of which He is the Saviour. Now as the church submits to Christ, so also wives should submit to their husbands in everything.

Husbands, love your wives, just as Christ loved the church and gave Himself up for her to make her holy, cleansing her by the washing with water through the word, and to present her to Himself as a radiant church, without stain or wrinkle or any other blemish, but holy and blameless.

In this same way, husbands ought to love their wives as their own bodies. He who loves his wife loves himself. After all, no one ever hated his own body, but he feeds and cares for it, just as Christ does the church—for we are members of His body. "For this reason a man will leave his father and mother and be united to his wife, and the two will become one flesh." This is a profound mystery—but I am talking about Christ and the church. However, each one of you also must love his wife as he loves himself, and the wife must respect her husband (Ephesians 5:21-33).

You may wonder how that is a restoration of mutuality.

I've heard that passage used over and over again to tell wives to knuckle under and obey their husbands and to tell husbands they have all the power in the marriage.

Is that really what the passage says? Let's look at it more closely.

Mutual Submission

I believe it is significant that Paul introduced his comments on marriage with the admonition, "Submit to *one another* out of reverence to Christ." Everything that follows is based on the premise that love for Christ would inspire husband and wife to a selfless devotion to each other. Each is to submit to the other, yield his or her will to the interests of the other. Elsewhere Paul wrote,

> *If you have any encouragement from being united with Christ, if any comfort from His love, if any fellowship with the Spirit, if any tenderness and compassion, then make my joy complete by being like-minded, having the same love, being one in spirit and purpose. Do nothing out of selfish ambition or vain conceit, but in humility consider others better than yourselves. Each of you should look not only to your own interests, but also to the interests of others (Philippians 2:1-4).*

The fact that Paul was not writing specifically about marriage serves only to underline the significance of these verses to marriage partners. If such attitudes and behavior are to characterize Christian relationships in general, how much more they should characterize marriage, potentially the most unified relationship of all!

In marriage, as in no other relationship, we have a responsibility to be sensitive and devoted to another's needs. We are to offer ourselves up to our spouse, allowing him or her to know us at the deepest level, in all our vulnerability, and trusting our mate to be loyal.

Power Plays in Courtship

Such a positive pattern of relating must begin in courtship. The decisions a couple makes during courtship—what they will talk about and what they will do—set the tone for the marriage that follows. How do they arrive at those decisions? Who has the power? Do they grant power to each other, or does each work to ensure it for himself or herself?

Perhaps the biggest decision made in courtship is how they will define their physical relationship. That decision, at its base, is one of power versus submission. Whose needs will be met? Whose standards will be observed? How much is too much? What is going to be right for both persons? Sadly, the decision is often made without discussion, and the precedent set has lasting effects.

Bill and Cindy started dating while they were both juniors at a Christian college. When it became known on campus that they were "a couple," Cindy was the envy of the women's dorm. Bill was a campus leader and was aiming for a prestigious career. He was a real catch, and everyone knew it, especially Cindy.

In fact, she could hardly believe that he was actually interested in her, and she directed all her efforts to keeping him interested. She worked hard to be everything he wanted and to satisfy his every whim. Seldom did she voice her own opinions and wishes. If by chance they ever did disagree, she deferred to Bill.

As the months passed, their relationship grew more intense, and they began to talk about marriage. Graduation and financial independence were a long way off, though, so Bill was reluctant to make any definite plans. Cindy understood his thinking, but felt insecure without some guarantee that they would actually get married.

Meanwhile, their physical relationship was progressing rapidly, and although they had never discussed how far they would go, they both passed limits they had set for themselves. Bill began telling Cindy that his love for her was so strong that he really needed the release of going to bed with her. Otherwise, he just didn't see how he could continue the relationship; it was too frustrating for him.

Cindy was torn between not wanting to violate her standards and not wanting to lose Bill. She kept her feelings to herself and for a short while evaded his demands, but she eventually gave in. Never did they talk about their individual needs and standards or try to decide what was going to be best for their relationship.

They did, finally, get married, and fifteen years later their marriage was crumbling. Since courtship days, Cindy had continued her pattern of trying to keep Bill happy by doing things his way. And he was very definite about what his way was. Silently she put up with his long hours at work and his weekends playing golf, and she went on fishing trips with him for their vacations.

The more she catered to him, the further they drifted apart. The harder Cindy worked to please him, and the more she gave in to his demands, the more Bill found himself despising her. It was a lopsided arrangement that satisfied no one. But neither Bill nor Cindy had a clear idea what was wrong.

Submission in Marriage

We hear a lot about the need for the wife to be submissive in marriage. Paul speaks of the wife's submission, and their *is* need for submission. But submission of what? To whom? Under what circumstances?

Cindy believed she was being properly submissive to Bill. But her way of submitting actually hindered rather than helped their relationship. What went wrong? Why wasn't it working?

Because, in fact, she was *not* being properly submissive to Bill. "Wives, submit to your husbands as to the Lord"— not "instead of to the Lord." Submission does not mean surrendering your integrity; you cannot give up your faith and violate what you believe to be true. You cannot discard your sense of self and write off all that you hold important. Giving yourself to another is not the same as obliterating your self. Submission is not subservience.

Neither is it being mild and compliant on the surface while unobtrusively pulling strings to get your own way— being the Submissive Concealer. That sort of covert control over another is self-serving rather than being committed to the good of the other.

Likewise, being helplessly dependent, abdicating your power and responsibility so that your mate is obligated to take care of your every need, is not being properly submissive either. That kind of helplessness is perhaps the most powerful stance a woman can take. In it, she exerts a control that serves neither her husband nor the relationship.

Although in Christian circles it is often the wife who takes on an overly submissive or pseudosubmissive role, husbands are not exempt. A man who feels a need to be taken care of will often choose a wife who is willing to take charge and allow the husband to abdicate his own responsibility in the marriage. Such a marriage becomes self-serving rather than mutually satisfying.

Submission means openness to the other's point of view as well as willingness to offer your opinion for consideration. It means sensitivity to your partner's needs and a determination to meet them in healthy, constructive ways—ways that will enhance rather than violate the sense of relationship between you. It means considering the other's interests as equal in value and importance to your own, but not denying your own.

Submission means trusting your mate's goodwill and ability to work through problems as you offer your own efforts to the problem-solving process. And it means being willing to be open enough to say what you need and then trusting your spouse to be concerned about those needs. When the two of you disagree about something and, after giving it your best effort, truly cannot come to a consensus (which is the ideal), then it's time for the wife to defer to her husband, and for him to accept the responsibility for his wife's welfare.

Above all, submission means being true to your own responsibility to the Lord, not abandoning your personality and convictions out of fear of conflict or disapproval. When you are motivated by such a fear you are actually acting out of self-interest, not true concern for your partner and for the relationship. But when you entrust yourself and your relationship to the Lord, maintaining your integrity and personhood, you are freed to truly give of the wealth that is you to your mate.

In the final analysis, when you abandon personal responsibility in favor of complying unthinkingly with another's wishes, you ignore the fact that each of us will some day give an account to God (Romans 14:13). A wife will not be able to say to the Lord, "He made me do it"; she will not be able to lay her choices to anyone's charge but her own.

Authority in Marriage
Paul gave his instructions to wives in the context of his prescription for the *whole marriage*. The wife's responsibility to respect her husband is complemented by the husband's responsibility to love his wife. Independent of the other, neither gives an accurate picture of the kind of marriage Paul was describing.

> *The husband is the head of the wife as Christ is the head of the church, His body, of which He is the Saviour. . . . Husbands, love your wives, just as Christ loved the church and gave Himself up for her. . . . Husbands ought to love their wives as their own bodies. He who loves his wife loves himself. After all, no one ever hated his own body, but he feeds and cares for it, just as Christ does the church (Ephesians 5:23, 25, 28-29).*

The passage is full of paradoxes. The husband is to be

the head—but he is to exercise his headship in the same life-giving way that Christ exercises His. He is to be in authority—but his authority is to be directed toward nurturing and caring for his wife as he would his own body. It is to be guided by love, and never used against his wife but on her behalf and on behalf of the relationship.

I believe the husband's role of authority can be as much misunderstood as the wife's role of submission. Authority is not authoritarianism, nor does it gain its strength from blind, absolute obedience. It consists not in control but in service and self-giving. In confronting a power struggle among His disciples, Christ said:

> *You know that the rulers of the Gentiles lord it over them, and their high officials exercise authority over them. Not so with you. Instead, whoever wants to become great among you must be your servant, and whoever wants to be first must be your slave—just as the Son of Man did not come to be served, but to serve, and to give His life as a ransom for many (Matthew 20:25-28).*

In the church's prescription for family structure, servant-leadership has at times been overlooked. Instead, the church has often favored a hierarchical notion of marriage, in which the husband takes the role of boss and the wife the role of underling. Such a view neglects the fact that through Christ, each of us is a priest before God in his or her own right (1 Peter 2:5; Revelation 5:10)—a truth for which the Protestant Reformers fought.

In addition, it distorts the original one-flesh design God intended for marriage and creates a triangle, wherein one partner has a special "in" with God and the other is excluded. It neglects the fact that God designed marriage to enhance the personhood of both husband and wife (Genesis 2:18) and to support their relationship—individually and together—with Himself.

I see misguided marriages in which a hierarchy is rigidly adhered to and where both partners are in pain. Reacting against the chaos of his own upbringing, and striving to fulfill what he sees as his responsibility, the husband adopts an authoritarian stance. He requires absolute obedience as he shoulders all the responsibility for the marriage and the family.

But certainly the crown sits heavy in such a relationship! He has no recourse but to be perfect—or at least to be seen as perfect, invulnerable, and infallible. Rather than sharing the depth of his life with his wife, letting her know his insecurities and inadequacies, the husband is isolated. He is not free to be human, to reveal needs or uncertainties or to show tenderness. If his wife or children dare to voice differing opinions or wishes, he feels threatened. Trapped in rigidly defined roles, his wife and his children are deprived of the kind of caring they need from him, and he misses out on the kind of support he needs from them. He returns to an aloneness worse than that experienced by Adam before Eve was created, since Adam at least had unbroken communion with God. The crown that man wears doesn't mean anything, because it doesn't satisfy his heart.

Husbands are not the only ones to get trapped in an authoritarian role. Sometimes a wife, also motivated by a need to cover her feelings of inadequacy, will take the dominant role in the marriage. To do so, she chooses a husband who will not challenge her but will yield his power to her. But although she gains the dominance she seeks, she does not satisfy her true needs, and the relationship suffers.

When either partner adopts an authoritarian role, closed to input from the other, intimacy withers. True intimacy requires the clear light of openness. It must let the other partner inside to embrace strengths and weaknesses, and to challenge those things that have been malformed. When marriage partners are not free to be whole persons relating intimately to each other, no one is satisfied; no one's needs are recognized and met.

Christ's Example

"Husbands, love your wives just as Christ loved the church" (Ephesians 5:25). How did Christ love the church? By giving Himself up for her, by meeting the deepest of all human needs, the need to be redeemed from sin. In all that—and because of all that—He maintained His authority. He is and always will be Lord. Yet His humility was such that He could say to His disciples, "I no longer call you servants, because a servant does not know his master's business. Instead, I have called you friends, for everything that I learned from My Father I have made known to you" (John 15:15).

Authoritarianism splits the relationship with secrets. One partner directs the life of another from an aloof, impenetrable position, shutting out the other's participation and input. Pseudosubmissiveness is secretive too. The reality of the supposedly submissive partner is carefully hidden from the other's view. Yet Christ said that the kind of relationship He wanted with His followers was one of complete openness—His openness to them, and their openness to Him.

Not only did Christ use His authority to bring His followers up to the position of friends and even co-heirs (Romans 8:17), but He did not cling jealously to His own status of equality with God. Instead He submitted Himself for their well-being. After Paul urged the Philippian Christians to build unity through mutual submission and caring (Philippians 2:1-4), he then pointed them to Christ's example.

Your attitude should be the same as that of Christ Jesus: who, being in very nature God, did not consider equality with God something to be grasped, but made Himself nothing, taking the very nature of a servant, being made in human likeness.

> *And being found in appearance as a man, He humbled Himself and became obedient to death—even death on a cross!*
>
> *Therefore God exalted Him to the highest place and gave Him the name that is above every name, that at the name of Jesus every knee should bow, in heaven and on earth and under the earth, and every tongue confess that Jesus Christ is Lord, to the glory of God the Father (Philippians 2:5-11).*

In Christ we see the perfect balance of authority and submission, exercised for the sake of intimacy with the ones He loves. His self-giving, His willingness to humble Himself and identify with the worst of the human condition, was the very basis of God's exalting Him "to the highest place."

Who Gets the Last Word?

Sinners that we are, none of us is capable of always reflecting the spirit of Christ in our interactions with each other. None of us is always properly submissive; none of us consistently uses power responsibly.

Yes, we *should* follow Christ's example in our relationship with each other. But even so, conflicts will arise. What then? Who should be the more submissive? Who gets the last word? Where does the ultimate responsibility lie?

In a healthy, thriving marriage, the relationship gets the last word. The relational process by which a man and woman interact with each other, expose vulnerabilities, and negotiate differences is the final court of appeal. The responsibility to meet each other on a feeling level and arrive at decisions in the context of their relationship goes far deeper than adhering to organizational structure or a set of rules. Ultimately, we are not responsible only to each other but to God. Keeping that eternal responsibility in mind does much toward tempering our selfish use of power.

More than any other human relationship, marriage provides the opportunity for mutual consensus and a true unity of spirit and purpose. Such unity does not consist merely in a husband and wife sifting through pros and cons but in their knowing intuitively, *We're in this together. We have lived together and shared enough that we know each other through and through. We can sense each other's desires, strengths, and needs. We can entrust ourselves to each other as we work together and negotiate our differences.*

In the sharing and negotiating, they resolve the paradoxes of authority—not by imposing a formula but by submitting to the needs of the relationship, that one-flesh unity that goes beyond the individuals involved.

It is not a process guaranteed to prevent hurts. Perfect solutions are not always attainable. Hurts are inevitable. But in the true relationship, the hurt is shared. Neither finds pleasure in beating the other down or joy in the other's pain.

In a fallen world, marriages will perhaps always have to have that fall-back position, the structure, to resort to when perfect consensus cannot be achieved. But if that structure is *all* a couple has to define their relationship, and they never learn to feel caringly with each other as they work through their differences with each other, their marriage will remain a caricature of what it was meant to be. It will be a rigid, empty shell rather than a living union energized by love.

n i n e

Navigating Change

After twelve years of saving and planning, Dave and Joyce were finally settling into their dream house when the news came. His company had just been bought out by a corporation on the East Coast, and the new owners were closing his office. Suddenly Dave and Joyce had to rethink their future.

Contrary to what the fairy tales would have us believe, getting married does not catapult us into a perpetually static happily-ever-after. One thing we can count on in this life is change—and the disruptions, problems, and feelings that go along with change. A spouse comes down with a chronic illness. Children are born, start school, become teenagers, leave home. The family moves to a new home. Husband and wife grow older and retire. A family member dies. The changes that occur in a marriage are endless, and no relationship or family is immune to them.

In addition to the changes that are a normal part of family life, the society around us is constantly changing, bombarding us with the need to respond, adapt. Families today face decisions that were unheard of a generation ago. Societal norms and values once thought unshakable have disappeared or been replaced.

Every change, whether it occurs inside or outside the family, whether it is sought or imposed, spells crisis to a marriage. A crisis is any occurrence that bears emotional significance to a couple and results in a change in their position or function. Crisis brings loss, stress, and the need to cope and adjust. Things a couple have come to expect and depend on are no longer, and they feel as if they are living in unfamiliar territory.

How a couple responds to a crisis, how they go about solving the problems and coping with the losses brought by change, affects the development of their marriage. Crisis builds on what is in a marriage and also reveals what is not there. It exposes the places where the bonding is not yet complete and strengthens the bond that already exists.

Changes—even those that are desired and chosen—are threatening. They require a couple to alter themselves or be altered, and that is scary. One or both of the partners are in a vulnerable spot, and sensitive communication, support, and faith in each other are vital but sometimes elusive. With our core of mistrust that we never quite discard, it is tempting to try to hide one's vulnerability and go back to dealing with life's difficulties alone.

Couples often come to me in the midst of a crisis. They are floundering because they don't know what to do; they care, but they are lost and overwhelmed. Old patterns of coping which they brought to the marriage from their own families aren't working anymore. They need to find new ways to think and behave, in order to deal with all the deep feelings that the crisis has triggered in them.

Over the years of working with couples, I've noticed four approaches that do *not* solve problems but, rather, compound them.

Postponing the Pain
Time will heal all ills. If we ignore what this change or problem is doing to us and refuse to feel the hurt it is

bringing, eventually it will go away.

Hoping that this is so, the spouses collaborate in a plan—spoken or unspoken—to deny the problem and carry on as if nothing has happened.

Some things do go away, but the feelings connected with them always resurface later. Any substantial problem will persist and show up over and over again. Issues that aren't looked at and dealt with but are locked away become sealed-off, no-trespassing areas. Because they aren't talked about, they take on the character of secrets.

When a child is having problems in school or among his playmates, the parents have to deal with it. Do they say, "It's just a phase. He'll grow out of it"? How do they know whether it is just a phase or if it is a problem they need to attend to?

A couple decides to make a major purchase that strains the limits of their budget—and then the hot water heater develops a leak. Bills and more bills come due, concrete evidence that certain choices have been made. How does the couple now deal with the consequences of those choices? Do they make adjustments, or do they continue as they always have, adding new debts to already burdened credit cards?

Part of denial is a mistrust of each other that eats away at the relationship. Couples who try to deny limitations and problems end up with a backlog of unresolved issues just waiting to burst out when a crisis comes along that refuses to be denied. The marriage can buckle under their weight.

Finding a Scapegoat
It's all their fault. If they (the government, the neighbors, the children, the relatives, God, or whoever else is handy) *hadn't done what they did, we wouldn't have problems.*

This is the old tactic of unifying against a common enemy. The couple avoids looking closely at themselves, each other, or the relationship by focusing on a "bad guy out there." And "out there" doesn't have to be very far away and may be within the family itself. It is not uncommon for children, or one child in particular, to become the scape-goat, carrying the blame for the parents' discomfort. Children are a disruption, a major change that upsets whatever equilibrium the marriage has attained. Thus they become "logical" targets, catching the brunt of marital distress.

Although on the surface the couple using this style looks united, even close, theirs is a hollow kind of closeness. Neither one dares be honest about fears or misgivings—especially those that have to do with the spouse. Each partner secretly feels that the other is to blame. But those feelings are driven underground, where they do what all secrets do—eat away at the core of the marriage. Neither partner is confident that the other, or the marriage, can withstand scrutiny and change. They both work to protect what they fear is a very fragile relationship that will crumble if dealt with directly. Finding a scapegoat is an anxious attempt to ensure their relationship.

It's those long hours my husband has to work. That's why we don't spend much time together. On the weekends we're busy with projects around the house, and we have so many responsibilities at church. Our problem is that we're just under too much pressure!

But does he *have* to work all those hours? Do all those projects *have* to take up all of every weekend? Are those church responsibilities ones the Lord has laid on them? In short, does the couple have anything to say about how their time is spent?

Obviously, they do. In blaming outside forces they seek to escape responsibility for their situation. But no one else can make their choices for them. If they are loaded down with obligations, it is because they have in some measure chosen to be. Naturally, there are sometimes extenuating circumstances that demand time and attention. Perhaps finances really are shaky enough that overtime work is temporarily necessary. But few situations are so rigid that a couple cannot have some control and choice in the matter.

Abdicating that responsibility is a way of avoiding looking at secret questions and fears. *Does he work those long hours so that he doesn't have to be with me? Do I keep myself busy on weekends because I'm afraid of the kind of closeness we might have if I didn't? Would we still love each other if we took a good look at each other? Would we be able to handle the changes we might find necessary?*

The distance a couple maintains through finding a scapegoat stands in the way of their bonding to each other. Although they maintain a united front, they feel an uncertainty that they are not dealing with. This uncertainty keeps their marriage in a perpetually tentative state. Its structure remains hollow, never being filled out with the substance of give-and-take from each other.

When they lose their scapegoat—for example, when the children leave home or the time for retirement comes—they are suddenly stranded in a crisis having to face each other for the first time in years. Now they can either get down to the work of really dealing with their marriage or they can run in panic. Most of us know of seemingly perfect couples who, for no reason apparent to an outsider, break up after years of marriage. Very often the split comes simultaneously with changes that force them finally to face each other without a third party to lean on. The safety they so carefully guarded for their marriage turns out to have been precarious indeed.

Blaming Your Spouse

If you didn't cut me down in public. . . . If you weren't such a spendthrift. . . . If you took better care of the house. . . . If it weren't for you, we'd have a perfect marriage!

Rather than look outside the marriage for a scapegoat, one partner blames the other for all their marital ills. But unless the accused partner is a masochist, such a style is doomed to be short-lived. Few husbands or wives are going to agree that they are to blame for all the problems in the marriage. Sooner or later, they will rebel—as well they should. When they do, the marriage may split, unless the blaming partner is willing to back up and take a look at his own responsibility in the relationship.

Taking the Blame
Some partners, however, *do* find it useful to take all the responsibility and to blame themselves for all the problems in the relationship.

If I weren't such a bad person, everything would be okay. You would be better off without me. This statement is made not only in words but sometimes in psychosomatic illnesses and even in suicide gestures. This attitude is a subtle abdication of responsibility. The person who assumes such a role and, perhaps, even uses it as a reason for leaving the relationship, is avoiding the responsibility of facing honestly what is going on inside—the anger or dissatisfaction toward the mate. Self-blame is an escape from dealing responsibly with the relational problems.

Taking all the blame is a very sneaky thing. It seems to have so much support, even from Scripture (although it is Scripture misread). *I'm such a sinner. It's all my fault. I'm supposed to look on others as better than myself—and they are! I'm no good at all!*

Such an approach can *seem* to hold the marriage together. But it keeps the two partners from communicating honestly with each other, and thus stands in the way of their closeness to one another.

If a self-blamer is married to someone whose appetite for intimacy is not very great, that partner may be content to have the other constantly taking the blame. Some husbands or wives will devote themselves to this weaker partner, trying desperately—and futilely—to nurture him or her out of such an apparently painful position. Others may be baffled, bewildered by this style of dealing with problems, feeling uncomfortable with it but not knowing how to counteract it.

Short-Term Gain, Long-Term Pain
These four styles of problem-solving possess certain attractions. They seem to provide a quick fix or, at least, an easy escape from the painful undertaking of finding an effective solution. Husband and wife can collaborate together in denial or in playing a blame game which, while seeming to be concerned with responsibility, actually sidesteps the hard work of carrying out their true responsibilities.

All the methods are geared toward finding a culprit. They offer simple, stylized answers to the problem, but no *solution*. They all look for ways to avoid the painful acknowledgment, "*We* have a problem that *we* need to deal with." In using these avoidance styles, a couple abandons faith in each other and in the Lord; they assume that they cannot deal with truth and that the Lord cannot guide them together into an effective solution. They run from honesty and intimacy with each other and with God.

Over the short term, these ways of dealing with problems are indeed easy. Pain is buried, responsibility is thrown onto a scapegoat, and the hard work of confronting and dealing with a problem directly is avoided. But what seems easiest over the short term is, over the long term, the hardest. Each time one of these coping styles is used, the marriage veers a little more off course, a little further into murky, dangerous waters. The marriage may last, but its progress toward maturity and stability is thwarted. Unresolved difficulties pile up and strain the relationship.

The best manner of dealing with problems is actually to do the hard work of taking them on as they come, calling them what they are, acknowledging responsibility for them, and making the changes called for, painful as they may be at the moment. This is the only way for the marriage bond to gain the strength it needs to withstand life's crises.

When Styles Clash
Spouses don't always agree on which faulty coping styles to employ. Sometimes they will want to use styles that

conflict with each other. We all have different backgrounds, and we approach problems the way we were taught to as we were growing up. Although few of us had actual lessons in problem-solving, we watched those around us, especially our parents, and we learned very significant things. If our family habitually used a defective coping style, we may have learned that pain was an evil that should be avoided at all costs. Or, that if one acknowledged responsibility for a problem, he would be permanently labeled a "bad guy." Or, that conflict was somehow dangerous or bad, and we could keep the family together by assuming the blame for everything ourselves.

We brought those lessons with us into marriage with the unconscious assumption that they reflected universally acknowledged truth. If our marriage partner learned similar or complementary lessons, a kind of peace will prevail in the marriage, even if the problems pile up unsolved. But if our husband or wife grew up learning a different style of problem solving, the result is conflict.

While this conflict might seem to be disastrous and destructive, it actually signals great hope for the marriage. What it destroys is the illusion of safety created by dishonest coping styles. If a husband and wife are comfortable with their way of dealing with problems, even if it is ineffectual, there is little hope that they will ever be motivated to change. But if the two have styles that clash and throw their relationship out of balance, both are likely to wake up to the fact that some kind of change is imperative. And that's where growth begins!

The couple must take another step in the process of separating from their original families. Each person needs to look at the style of problem-solving he or she brought to the marriage and say, "Perhaps this isn't the only right way; maybe my family didn't have the whole truth. I need to listen to what you say, because you might have some of the truth too. Or, maybe we need to try together to find a new way of dealing with the changes and difficulties that life brings us—a way neither of us has ever known before."

In the negotiation of those differences something new is born—not just a different manner of solving problems, but a new character to their marriage. The relationship becomes uniquely their own, not a clone of their parents' marriages.

Yes, the clash of styles is painful. It brings stress and distress and anxiety. But it is a functional anxiety. If their marriage is important to them, the couple will be motivated by anxiety to find new ways to relate to each other in order to create a more wholesome marriage. They can each come out from behind their protective shelters and relate to one another as real people, with real hurts and needs and with unique contributions to make to their marriage. They can learn to trust each other at a new level as they risk giving up their fears and prejudices and letting intimacy blossom. It is this intimacy that gives real strength to their marriage, not the superficial togetherness achieved by collaborating to avoid problems.

Navigating Change

Yes, change is inevitable and often uncomfortable—even painful. In the face of change we find ourselves stripped of reliable props and we feel vulnerable. But hiding will not give us the security we seek. It is only as we overcome our intimidation, venture out of our self-protectiveness, and work through the difficulties arm in arm with our spouse that we find true safety and strength.

A husband loses his job. Perhaps it was due to circumstances beyond his control; perhaps it was due to his own failure in performance. Either way, he feels alone, vulnerable, perhaps angry or guilty. He may even wonder whether the Lord is still with him and in control. Self-doubt creeps in, and he expects his wife to doubt him too.

But rather than withdraw from her to nurse his own wounds, he needs to turn to her and allow her to participate in the process of dealing not only with the external change but also with all the internal ramifications of that change. He must forfeit the option to go it alone and allow her to come close to him and walk with him through the difficulties. He must tell her honestly about his feelings of sadness, anger, guilt, and fear. He must choose to trust that she still has faith in him and wants to enter caringly into his experience with empathy and support.

As he shares with his wife, he should remember that she will have her own set of emotions in response to this crisis. He must be open to her expressions of disappointment, frustration, and apprehension, empathizing with her rather than being defensive.

For her part, his wife must be faithful to her husband's trust and not let him down, no matter what she is feeling in this time of change. But she must not hide her feelings. Her husband knows they are there, for the change affects both of them. She too needs to be honest about what is going on inside of her, acknowledging her own hurt and uncertainty—though without blaming her husband or taking his losses as a personal affront—as she joins him in dealing with this disruption in their lives. She must demonstrate a faith in him that says, "I've seen you go through other difficulties and losses, and you've made it. I'm confident that you will make it again, and I'm with you in this. I'll be honest with you about what it does to me and what my needs and hopes are, but I will not try to make you feel guilty or tell you how you should act. I will not make demands on you. Rather, I will trust you to do what you need to do to deal with this problem. I may not be able to solve your problem, but I'm available to help you in it."

Together they can take their situation to the Lord, renewing their confidence in His goodness and sovereignty, keeping Him in the center of the circle of their marriage. They can be as honest with Him as they are with each other, trusting Him to care about their feelings and their circumstances. God's people have never been immune to trouble, but they have always had His presence as a resource. As Paul wrote, "Who shall separate us from the love of Christ? Shall trouble or hardship or persecution or famine or nakedness or danger or sword?...No, in all these things we are more than conquerors through Him who loved us" (Romans 8:35, 37).

Even if the job loss was due to some personal failure on the husband's part, the issue for their marriage is whether there will still be loyalty. It is something they both must choose—she to be loyal and he to merit that loyalty by being willing to sort out whatever was personal failure and then to work on it. Perhaps he was not up to the requirements of the job. Should he seek further training? Or should he look at himself and say, "This really is me. I don't really have the skills or gifts that job calls for, but I have others. I can get another job that calls for the particular strengths I have." Sometimes such a change will result in less income. Can husband and wife together adapt to that? They may need to reexamine their values and look at the basis for their identities.

In the face of life's problems and changes, both husband and wife are vulnerable. Both are hurting and they need one another. They cannot afford to turn against each other with mistrust and recriminations. If the problem involves both of them, they should arrive at the solution together. If it involves only one of them directly, they still need to be together emotionally as the one partner makes the adjustments that the change calls for.

Not every situation has an ideal solution. Sometimes it is virtually impossible to find a new job with a salary equivalent to the old one. Sometimes an illness cannot be cured. Sometimes losses are irreversible. Together both partners must acknowledge the limitations they face and say, "Well, here we are. Where does this leave us? What *can* we do? How do we accept our personal limits without limiting our experience of love and loyalty?" Whatever the external losses, they do not have to be experienced internally. The marriage does not have to be depleted; in fact, their bond can be strengthened even in tragedy if they work at it.

The marriage that thrives even through difficulties is a priceless gift, not only to the marriage partners but to their children as well. Parents must not try to shield their children from the realities of life. The children will know, at least intuitively, that something is different or amiss. If they're not included at some level in the process of dealing with the problem, they will wonder if they are at fault, especially if they are very young. They need to be reassured that they are not, and they should be encouraged to express their fears. They also need to feel sure that their father and mother are equal to the task of meeting life's difficulties and that the marriage is trustworthy and strong, in spite of outward circumstances.

Where Does It All End?

As long as you are married you will encounter changes and problems. People often speak of the first few years of marriage as being full of adjustments. In truth, the adjustments never end. Children come and leave. Finances wax and wane. The forced activities of the middle years give way to the unstructured time of retirement. Our bodies age and weaken. And finally, we must face death—our own or our partner's—and navigate that change together. Each stage of life leads into the next, with its unique stresses and challenges. In one sense, we never "arrive."

Yet, in another sense, we do. Each stage of life successfully navigated is another milestone on the way to maturity. Its lessons become a resource of wisdom for coping with the new circumstances and stresses that arise. It is a wisdom that not only strengthens us but is passed on to others—our children, the church, the community.

There is a richness that accrues from meeting problems together. We are satisfied as we watch our children being born, growing up, and leaving home ready to make lives for themselves. Our confidence increases as we consider the financial gains and setbacks that we have managed; we know that our security lies elsewhere. We remember the difficulties and tragedies and knòw that we have not been defeated but have found strength through them.

We look back with increasing appreciation at the ways our mate has contributed not only to the marriage but to who we are. As we consider what we have been through and the maturity we have gained, we feel a sharper awareness of the Lord's participation in our lives and a firmer confidence that we will continue to journey into blessing, no matter what the hazards along the way. We spend a lifetime navigating change together. And where does it get us? To the solid ground of a virtually unshakable marriage.

The Apostle Paul knew about this process. In fact, he wrote about it as a norm of the Christian life.

Therefore, since we have been justified through faith, we have peace with God through our Lord Jesus Christ, through whom we have gained access by faith into this grace in which we now stand. And we rejoice in the hope of the glory of God. Not only so, but we also rejoice in our sufferings, because we know that suffering produces perseverance; perseverance, character; and character, hope. And hope does not disappoint us, because God has poured out His love into our hearts by the Holy Spirit, whom He has given us (Romans 5:1-5).

That's where it ends—with a hope based on our own experience with each other and with the Lord. A hope that can be confidently passed on to our children as they venture out on their own. A hope that is the reward for battles met head-on and won. A hope that strengthens us as we meet that final great change, death. A hope that stabilizes our marriage and makes it truly worthwhile.

t e n

Sexuality: Celebrating the Bond

D rive down any American highway and look at the
billboards, and you will see it. Browse through the
magazines at the checkout in any supermarket, and
it's there. Flip on the television, any channel, any hour of
the day. The message comes through loud and clear: we
are a nation preoccupied with sex.

Since the late 1960s and early 1970s, Western culture has
congratulated itself on being sexually liberated. Traditional
boundaries and limitations on sexual expression have been
declared obsolete; consenting adults are now "free" to engage in any sexual activity they want.

But are we really free? Our national preoccupation with
sex would suggest that actually we're as self-conscious as
ever about this aspect of our lives. While the old constraints against sexual expression may have diminished, in
their place are demands for performance and appearance
that past generations seldom had to worry about. And relationships are no better off for the change—if divorce statistics are any indication.

Erica Jong, whose novels have capitalized on supposedly
liberated sexuality, wrote recently in *Ms.:*

> *Our society has had a decade and a half of experi-*
> *mentation with random sexual freedom. We have*
> *discovered that it is neither so very sexy nor so very*
> *free. My generation is disillusioned with sex as a*
> *social panacea. We look longingly at the marriages of*
> *our parents and grandparents and wonder how on*
> *earth they managed to stay best friends for so long—*
> *or even worst friends for so long! But at least they*
> *had someone to read the newspaper with.*"

A telling commentary on where sexual permissiveness has brought us! In seeking to have it all, sexually speaking, we have forfeited both enduring relationships and sexual satisfaction. Instead of liberty we have granted ourselves license—and are as confused and lonely as ever.

Sex from the Inside Out

Whether our preoccupation with sex is prudish or libertine, we will always be confused and dissatisfied if we separate sexuality from the relationship meant to be its context. Sex was never intended to be satisfying as a merely physical activity. It may be physically gratifying, but by itself it cannot fill the deep human hunger for intimacy.

We were created as sexual beings: "God created man in His own image, in the image of God He created him; male and female He created them" (Genesis 1:27). Human sexuality was inherent in the goodness of God's design and creation of the world, and is part of the image of God that we bear. Fundamental to the relationship a man and woman are to have with each other in marriage, it sets marriage apart from all other relationships.

But over and over again, people manage to miss the goodness of sex, either denying it completely or distorting it into something it was never meant to be. Rather than expressing the heart of marital joy, sex too often is at the heart of marital discord, ranking with money as the issue most frequently fought about in marriage.

Many have tried to find ways to correct this problem area in marriage. The popular press abounds with advice about how to achieve better sex. The reasoning goes that if things are good in bed, the rest of the marriage will be fine. Sex is identified as glue that can hold a marriage together. Get the technique right and marital bliss will follow.

But they've got it inside out. Good sex doesn't keep marriage together. Rather, a good marriage keeps sex alive. It's the intimate bond between a husband and wife that provides the security for free sexual expression. Physical intimacy flourishes when dependable love and commitment surround it. A good sexual relationship is produced more outside the bedroom than in. Its development depends on the day-to-day interaction between a husband and wife as they work together to negotiate differences, deal with problems, and solidify the bonding between them.

Back to the Bond
Ellie and Ben seemed like a model couple, but they had a problem no one could see—and that they couldn't talk about. By day they went about the normal routines of the typical married couple, but night after night went by with no physical contact between them. They had each read articles in popular magazines about sexual technique and satisfaction, but the articles had just made Ellie and Ben feel more confused, frustrated, and inadequate.

In reality, Ellie and Ben knew all they needed (if not more than they needed) about sexual technique. That wasn't their problem. And their difficulty wasn't in their physiology, either. They were both physically in good working order. Their problem lay not in their bodies but in their bonding.

What Ellie and Ben overlooked is the fact that sexuality, and the sexual relationship in marriage, does not have to do only with the act of intercourse. A couple may have difficulties with that, but the core of the problem usually lies in their emotional lives rather than in their bodies. At its root, sexuality is as much emotional as physical.

Behind the outward, physical expression of love between a man and woman is the whole history of their relationship with each other. And behind that is the history of each of them as individuals, and what they learned about relationships and bonding over the years.

The bonding that goes on in marriage owes a great deal to the kind of bonding that each partner experienced in infancy and childhood. Sexuality, as part of that bonding, thus also bears marks of that heritage. The toddler learns to carry within himself all that his parents are to him, and to find comfort and confidence in their memory when they are away. What he has internalized from his parents sustains the relationship with them when he is alone; it explodes into joy when he is reunited with them.

In the same way, a married couple, as they are bonding with each other, learn to carry each other inside. When they are successful at this, the relationship they have with each other will persist, even through absences.

Fantastic Sex

In recent years, much has been made of people's sexual fantasies, the erotic daydreams they spin. But those daydreams are not worthy of the label of sexuality when they focus only on physical images. Sex is, first and foremost, a *relationship*. It's not about bodies and physical sensation; it's about persons venturing into intimacy with each other. That intimacy is made up of all of a man's and woman's experiences and interactions with each other and the ways they have learned to lovingly carry each other inside. That internal image is at the heart of true sexual fantasy. Underlying it all is an incessant drive for oneness—not merely physical but emotional and spiritual as well.

A husband and wife develop fantasies of each other, but that does not mean that their imaginations conjure up pictures different from what appears in the real world. Instead, the fantasy begins to capture the essence of the other person, seeing him or her in all the depth and beauty that is there, and letting him or her become a part of oneself. The fantasy includes the physical image of the spouse but it doesn't stop there. The physical image is only a part of the larger image of that person as a whole. Through fantasy, the sexual relationship becomes an outgrowth of the whole process of a man and woman incorporating each other into their lives and bonding with each other.

There is a myth abroad that women need this emotional, relational component more than men do in order to find sexual satisfaction; and that when it comes to sex, men are interested primarily in physical gratification and can do without the emotional base.

That is a gross misconception. Adam didn't need Eve primarily for physical satisfaction; he needed a mate with whom to bond. Eve solved his problem of aloneness, not his sexual frustration. Men in our culture often disguise their need for tenderness, but it is there, nonetheless. Look at the great literature of the world. Who is responsible for the bulk of the world's great love poetry? Mostly men. Or look at the history of chivalry or of male jealousy and conflict over women. That was not merely a show of bravado or machismo; it reflected men's emotional needs for relationship as deep as any woman's.

We are so easily confused about how to think and feel about sex. Fortunately, the One who gave us the gift of sexuality in the first place also left us an illustration in Scripture of what sex can be to us.

The Song of Solomon is a beautiful record of the love a man and woman can feel for each other. The lover's fantasies of his beloved are interwoven with her fantasies of him in one of the world's greatest love songs. Their words describe the physical love between them, yet the song is striking for its absence of lewdness. The essence of their fantasies is not physical sensuality. Instead, the strong love and honor in which they hold each other pulses underneath and gives vibrancy to their physical enjoyment of each other. They yearn for each other as persons; their bodies are the vehicles for expressing their love for each other. Their fantasies of each other—the images of each other that they carry inside—ache for expression in physical union, not as an end in itself but as a demonstration of their deep, internal bonding with each other. The beloved says,

> *Like an apple tree among the trees of the forest*
> * is my lover among the young men.*
> *I delight to sit in his shade,*
> * and his fruit is sweet to my taste.*
> *He has taken me to the banquet hall,*
> * and his banner over me is love.*
> *Strengthen me with raisins,*
> * refresh me with apples,*
> * for I am faint with love.*
> *His left arm is under my head,*
> * and his right arm embraces me. . . .*
> *My lover is mine and I am his;*
> * he browses among the lilies.*
>
> *Until the day breaks*
> * and the shadows flee,*
> *turn, my lover*
> * and be like a gazelle*
> *or like a young stag*
> * on the rugged hills.*
> *All night long on my bed*
> *I looked for the one my heart loves. . . .*
> *My lover is radiant and ruddy,*
> * outstanding among ten thousand. . . .*
> *His mouth is sweetness itself;*
> * he is altogether lovely.*
> *This is my lover, this my friend,*
> * O daughters of Jerusalem.*
> *(Song of Songs 2:3-6, 16–3:1; 5:10, 16)*

You have stolen my heart, my sister, my bride;
  you have stolen my heart
with one glance of your eyes,
  with one jewel of your necklace.
How delightful is your love, my sister, my bride!
  How much more pleasing is your love than wine,
  and the fragrance of your perfume than any
    spice! . . .
Sixty queens there may be,
  and eighty concubines,
  and virgins beyond number;
but my dove, my perfect one, is unique (Song of
Songs 4:9-10; 6:8-9).

If sex were only physical, any body would satisfy. But it's not. It has to do with the deep longing of two people for each other as unique individuals, wholly and exclusively, in intimate bonding. Sexual fantasy, when attended to, chafes to be expressed in active demonstration of the love it carries.

Feeding the Fantasy

Sex was designed to be a means of deep communion between a husband and wife; the fantasies they have of each other and the attraction they hold for each other are a part of the original, God-given design. In a healthy marriage, their fantasies are not only physical, but reflect an image of the whole person. As the years go by, these images of each other become more defined as the couple interact with each other and forge their bond. They encounter problems in life and work together to overcome them, and in so doing build mutual respect. They open themselves up to each other and share their vulnerability, and gain trust as they experience each other's empathy and caring. They affirm their exclusive loyalty to one another as they let go of their families, and experience the sweetness of holding fast to each other. As their relationship deepens, so does their sexual attraction. As long as their bond is growing, so is their sexual relationship.

In a culture that worships youth and beauty, it is easy to miss the essence of true sexuality and focus merely on the externals. But what is left in such relationships after youth and beauty have faded? Little, if that is what the relationship was based on. When the novelty wears off and aging becomes more and more a fact of life, the fantasy is kept alive by all kinds of nonsexual things—respect, honor, loyalty, empathy, caring, honesty, openness—the ingredients of true intimacy. Their attractiveness to each other transcends bodily appeal. Their fantasy or imaging of one another is multidimensional.

When they come together in loving, physical union, it is not merely the exposure of their bodies but the exposure of their selves that renews the bond between them. Secrets and barriers have been cast away. What remains is solidly grounded trust in each other's character, caring, and unconditional acceptance.

George and Vera have been married almost forty years. They have raised three children, pulled up roots and household for two cross-country moves, weathered financial setbacks and recoveries, and buried their parents. They have been through a lot together and have the gray hairs and wrinkles to prove it.

Somehow, though, they don't seem to have caught on yet to the idea that they are growing older, that their "best years" are behind them, that they should no longer be attracted to each other or excited by each other. In fact, they rather agree with Robert Browning's sentiment, "Grow old along with me! The best is yet to be." George's eyes still twinkle admiringly when he looks at Vera across a room. Vera still likes to snuggle up next to George for a long chat. Through the years they let each other into more and more rooms in their lives. Few doors remain shut between them, and fewer still are locked. They know each other inside out and have no illusions—and no regrets.

Their grandchildren laugh at the way they tease and flirt and hug each other, but it is a laugh of enjoyment and security in the rightness of the relationship. They hope they will still be as much in love when they have been married forty years.

What is their secret? Some may think George and Vera were just lucky to have married "the right one." But they *worked* for what they have with each other. They invested time, energy, and most important, their very selves in the process of building a lasting, love-filled union.

Barriers in the Bedroom

Bonding in marriage takes time and effort to develop, and the process is seldom smooth. All that is sinful in us, all that defends against closeness and being known and sharing ourselves, pulls against it even as we are driven toward it. It is not surprising, then, that the sexual relationship between a husband and wife will experience the same ups and downs as their emotional bonding. A couple's sexual relationship must develop and grow just as every other aspect of their marriage does.

In many ways, it is a mirror of every aspect of their relationship, as it demonstrates the kind of sharing and empathy they have developed between them. It tests their negotiation of differences, valuing of each other's feelings, and trust in each other's character. It declares their loyalty to each other.

• Relational barriers. Whatever is wrong outside the bedroom shows up inside the bedroom as well. Are there secrets that distance them from each other? The couple carries that distance to bed with them. Is one doubting the other's loyalty and caring? The doubt cannot be shelved at bedtime. Is one failing to honor the other—perhaps by speaking disparagingly of faults? That one will not honor the partner in bed either.

The list can go on. I am convinced that God designed the intimacy of the sexual relationship as an accurate gauge of how the rest of the relationship is going. Are there problems in bed? Ninety-nine percent of the time they have been brought to bed from the total relationship.

I do not deny that sexual problems can at times have physiological roots. But in my practice I have seen that the most common cause of sexual problems is that spouses have become strangers to each other. Secrets have sprung up and been left untended. Their trust in each other has eroded, and with it their intimacy. Without openness, caring, and trust, the sexual relationship cannot subsist, especially when the external factors of youth and beauty are wearing thin. The sexual bond grows from spiritual unity, reinforced by their mutual prayer and sharing.

• Physical barriers. But what about truly physiological problems? Especially as we age, these can intrude into a sexual relationship. Diabetes can cause impotence, as can tumors or prostate surgery. If these difficulties are not curable, a sexuality that goes beyond a merely physical relationship is most important.

However, irreversible physical problems are rare. Most of them can be dealt with so that if all is well in other areas of the relationship, sexual relations can be enjoyed even into old age. Impotence resulting from alcoholism may be reversed and controlled. Physical discomfort due to a deficiency of estrogen in menopausal women can be treated. The enjoyment of sexuality can usually last as long as the marriage.

• Historical barriers. Sometimes disruptions in the bonding process, and thus in the growth of sexual enjoyment, have their roots in a history of abuse, particularly sexual abuse. This can be true particularly for women. According to a recent FBI report, one out of three girls who are now twelve years old will be raped or molested by the time they reach adulthood. One thing this statistic means is that more and more women are entering marriage with a sexual experience that has been physically agonizing and emotionally devastating. Women—and men—who have been violated sexually must overcome emotional pain and revulsion associated with sex before they can be free to give themselves without reservation to a sexual relationship in marriage—or for that matter, to the emotional bond that fosters the sexual relationship.

Even without sexual abuse, many individuals have experienced physical and emotional abuse that likewise forms barriers to bonding. Those who were abused often have difficulty trusting others and forming close relationships. Poor self-image, an almost inevitable by-product of abuse, prevents them from feeling worthy of love or believing they have anything valuable to give to a relationship. Naturally, such feelings will have a great impact on a couple's ability to be sexually intimate.

The barriers raised by a history of abuse are formidable but not insurmountable. Talking about one's experiences and fears with one's spouse and, if necessary, a caring counselor, can bring healing and freedom. The love and security of a good marriage can be a vehicle of redemption even when there has been profound pain and violation of trust.

• Barriers of ignorance. The sexual revolution may have changed the way our society behaves sexually, but apparently it has done little to revolutionize our true understanding of sex. Misconceptions abound, often propagated by the media. Though sex is talked about freely, we cannot assume that couples enter marriage with realistic expectations about their sexual relationship. For every bit of accurate information they possess, they are as likely to carry several mistaken ideas or impressions garnered from sources ranging from movies to air-brushed photos to television talk-show hosts.

The popular media tends to present only one view of sex: the "10" body and nonstop physical ecstasy. When young couples enter marriage expecting their physiques and performance automatically to match those images, they are set up for disappointment. Frustrated, they may give up before they've even had a chance to develop a sensitive, loving, mutually satisfying physical relationship.

Nor are newlyweds the only ones at risk. The long-married couple who have enjoyed a sexual relationship for years may not be aware, as they enter middle age, how physiological changes can be affecting them. If they begin to need more time for arousal, husband and wife may mistakenly blame themselves or their spouse for a lack of desire or love. They may begin to fear their relationship is at risk when actually all they need is to give themselves more time and understanding.

Dismantling the Barriers

Any or all of these barriers may be operative in a couple's life. In a society that frowns on sexual hangups, it is tempting to look for a quick fix when sexual problems arise. But remember, *sex is first of all a relationship, not a performance or a commodity.* The barriers that are encountered are not to be leaped over and left quickly behind, but are to be gently dismantled, piece by piece, and re-formed as pathways to intimacy. The solutions are not to be discovered body to body but person to person, in the safety and love of marriage. There is no substitute for talking about the problems, as openly as possible, and jointly taking responsibility for working them through.

I remember a young couple who ran into difficulties early in their marriage. Both were from highly protected backgrounds that discouraged any discussion of sex. The impression they got was that sex was somehow dirty, and that truly spiritual people never let themselves be contaminated by even thinking about it.

As teenagers, they naturally had thoughts, feelings, and questions about sex, but they were afraid they would be condemned if they verbalized them. So, being normal teenagers, they kept their mouths shut and their eyes and ears open. Unfortunately, since church and family were silent on the issues of sexuality, the information they picked up, courtesy of peers and secular media, was virtually devoid of moral or interpersonal values.

With that background they entered marriage, and were dismayed to find that sex was awkward, sometimes painful, and always dissatisfying. Obedient to the dicta of their past, though, they kept quiet and never ventured to talk about the problems they were encountering. They didn't know whether to blame themselves or each other, and secretly did some of both. They ended up feeling alienated, resentful, and ashamed.

In the midst of their sexual confusion and disillusionment, the young wife was suddenly swept off her feet by a charming older man at her workplace. He was divorced and experienced, and as one thing led to another, he introduced her to sexual pleasures she hadn't thought possible.

Eventually the affair was discovered, almost shattering the already fragile marriage. Fortunately, their backgrounds had instilled in them a strong sense that divorce was not to be considered. So they reluctantly and fearfully sought the help of a marriage therapist who helped them piece their relationship back together.

In the process they each discovered pieces of themselves they hadn't known existed. As they learned to talk and share those pieces with each other, they began to appreciate how truly complex a marriage relationship is. They became aware of their individual sexual needs and desires, and learned to grant themselves permission to have those needs and desires and to communicate them to each other. The sensitivity and depth that was added to their relationship was beautiful to see, as was the forgiveness that gradually displaced the hurt and resentment that had accumulated both from the affair and from their earlier marital struggles.

False Fantasies
When couples do not confront and resolve sexual problems in marriage, they are in danger of turning to unhealthy

practices. We all have a God-given capacity for sexuality
and the fantasy that goes with it. The ability to think and
feel sexually is not a product of sin; it was built into man
before the Fall. But, like everything else in our lives, our
sexuality was infected when sin entered.

As sin strikes at the heart of relationship, one of its
effects is the perverse capacity for separating sexuality
from the deep relationship for which it was intended. Just
as the roots of healthy sexuality lie in our fantasy, so fantasy can be employed in unhealthy sexuality that violates
God's original design.

Our Lord knew the dangers inherent in the illicit use of
fantasy. In Matthew 5:27-28 we have a record of Jesus'
words, "You have heard that it was said, 'Do not commit
adultery.' But I tell you that anyone who looks at a woman
lustfully has already committed adultery with her in his
heart."

Was Jesus saying that to be aware of a sexual drive and
of the sexual attractiveness of someone who is not your
marriage partner is the same as committing adultery? Some
who have thought so have condemned the awareness of
another's attractiveness in themselves and in others. When
they have found themselves responding to another person's
attractiveness, they have prayed that their feelings would
go away, and have fed on guilt and self-contempt when
they didn't.

I don't believe God will ever say yes to such a prayer. We
may as well ask that our sense of smell or our capacity for
logic be taken away. God has made us with a healthy ability to be aware of sexual attractiveness.

If sexual awareness is not sinful, what was Jesus warning against? The word *lust* is very interesting when you
look at its meaning in Greek, the language in which Jesus'
words were recorded. The word *epithumeo* means to long
for (rightfully or otherwise) and to desire deeply. Jesus
used a form of the same word of Himself when He said, "I
have eagerly desired (*epithumia*) to eat this Passover with

you [His disciples] before I suffer" (Luke 22:15). The word, in itself, has no sexual connotation; it simply expresses the intensity of longing and desire.

So when Jesus warned against looking at a woman lustfully, I do not believe that He was condemning the mere acknowledging of another's attractiveness. Sexual awareness is a sign that we are functioning as we were created to, in a way that fits us for married love.

What Jesus was condemning was the illicit *fantasy*—not just seeing someone as attractive but desiring to have a person to whom we are not married. Jesus was warning us against dwelling on the desire, cultivating it, contemplating its object, imagining and coveting its fulfillment. We are to guard ourselves from crossing the line from merely appreciating someone's attractiveness to beginning to look for ways to develop a sexual liaison.

In 2 Samuel 11 we read the account of King David's fall into adultery with Bathsheba. "One evening David got up from his bed and walked around on the roof of the palace. From the roof he saw a woman bathing. The woman was very beautiful, and David sent someone to find out about her" (vv. 2-3).

David's downfall was not in regarding Bathsheba as beautiful. Had he gone down from the roof and thought no more about the incident, he probably would have escaped the serious trouble that followed. His downfall was that in finding Bathsheba beautiful, he decided to procure her for himself; his desire for her demanded satisfaction.

In commenting on Jesus' equation of lustful looking and actual adultery, R.V.G. Tasker summarizes, "Adultery is but the final expression of lustful thoughts harbored in the imagination and fed by the illicit contemplation of the object of desire, so that the lust of the eyes and the lust of the flesh cannot be dissociated."[7] In other words, Jesus could equate lust with adultery because, in fact, lust, when it is fed and developed, *becomes* adultery. The sexual relationship is the outworking of the fantasy.

Adultery shatters. It is the one thing that our Lord allowed as just cause to dissolve a marriage. After an affair, the legalities of divorce are but an echo of a fact already stated: the trust has been violated, the loyalties betrayed, the caring trampled. Forgiveness and reconciliation are possible but costly.

When we think of adultery, we tend to think only of a man or woman forming a clandestine sexual relationship with a partner of the opposite sex. But *any* extramarital sexual activity or liaison—be it incest, homosexual behavior, child abuse, submersion in pornography or any other—severs the marital bond. It takes the gift of sexuality and wrenches it from the context in which it was meant to be used. Instead of celebrating the marital bond, it rejects it in favor of another kind of relationship. It abandons marital intimacy in favor of self-gratification.

Celebrate!

"Marriage should be honored by all, and the marriage bed kept pure, for God will judge the adulterer and all the sexually immoral" (Hebrews 13:4). Why the warning? Because God is against sexual freedom and pleasure? On the contrary, because God is *for* sexual freedom and pleasure—the freedom and pleasure that can flower only in the nurturing soil of a solid, committed marriage.

The sexual relationship between a man and a woman is a tangible demonstration that marriage is different, more intimate than any other relationship can possibly be. The bond it celebrates is one that is to be treasured not only because God commands it to be, but because that command was designed for our ultimate good and satisfaction. As a husband and wife give themselves freely and exclusively to each other in a sexual relationship, they are affirming the unique and special place each holds in the other's heart, and are preserving a unity that demonstrates God's own love. And this is certainly something to celebrate!

e l e v e n

Partners in Parenting

James drifted into the youth group meeting one blustery October night and hung around on the fringe of activity most of the evening. The youth pastor noticed him and made a point to encourage him to come back. He did, and gradually began forming friendships in the group.

He seemed particularly drawn to the youth pastor and frequently lingered after the meetings or outings to talk. Bit by bit James' story spilled out—the years of hostility between his parents, the nights lying awake listening to the fighting and banging that rose up from his parents' room downstairs, the agony of feeling called on to choose sides between them, the gnawing fear that somehow he was responsible for all the upheaval in his house. Now, at last, they were getting a divorce, putting a seal of finality on the enmity between them, and James felt as if the earth were crumbling beneath him. What little stability he had known in the midst of his family's upheavals was dissolving, and he was scared.

The youth group, with the relationships it offered with peers and particularly with this caring, solid adult, was a haven to which he steered himself with relief. He eventually found a relationship even more stabilizing—with the Lord—and the whole church rallied around this refugee from family war with support and succor, congratulating itself on having rescued him.

But James was not new to this church. His parents had attended sporadically while he was growing up, and he had been in and out of Sunday School during his grade-school years. His family had been in trouble then too. Various Sunday School teachers had known it but had felt reluctant to intrude. It took the crisis of divorce before church members were willing to intervene.

The ravages of divorce are tearing up our children, and the church is falling down in its responsibility to families. Very often, as in James' case, the church comes through with flying colors *after* the family collapses; and that is good, as far as it goes. But it doesn't go far enough. The most sympathetic pastor, youth leader, Sunday School teacher, or church member can never be more than make-shift support, an inadequate substitute for the incomparable foundation of a child's knowing that his father and mother can weather conflicts, change, and the problems of life and come out not only smiling but with caring and with deeper communication and trust.

The church needs to come to the aid not only of the survivors of a family that has crashed but to the family itself, *before* it crashes. It needs to speak not just to the individual who has been pulled out of a bad situation, but to the bad situation. I don't hold any illusions that the church can always move in on a family in trouble and turn the situation around. But it does have a responsibility to see the *whole* family as a system, seeking to meet its needs rather than waiting to pick up the pieces when the system collapses. The best way to serve the children is to serve the family—support it, encourage it, offer it hope, motivate it to survive and find healing.

Unfortunately, in this day of rising divorce, I sense the opposite trend. Just when children most need the church to speak out for the stability of the family, the church is relaxing and compromising and sometimes even condoning divorce. It has accepted the rationalization that the highest good is what feels good, and if a marriage no longer *feels* good, it can be let go. Much of the church has acquiesced to the notion that the pain of hard work on a relationship need not be borne. It has accepted the standard of good feelings as the confirmation of God's will and of personal experience as the hallmark of faith. While parents are finding relief from relational pains by shedding their marriages, children are bearing the battle scars of a war that is not theirs.

What children need more than anything else, in order to grow into healthy, loving adults, is to have parents who have been able to develop a caring, committed bond between them. No other situation offers quite the same gifts to the growing child.

Gifts of a Good Marriage

• Love between equals. Watch any healthy baby beginning to discover its surroundings. Have you ever wondered what goes on behind those wide-open eyes as he soaks in his environment? Even before he has language, he is beginning to form impressions and struggling to make sense of what he sees, hears, and feels. There is no escaping his gaze, no camouflaging what is going on in the family, no way to lie or cover up to him. He is learning without words, and what he learns will stay with him as a foundation for life. Even after he learns to talk, his powers of observation will be adding to his understanding of life and relationships.

If his parents have learned to share, empathize, work together in solving problems, and care for each other as equals, the child will learn this kind of love. He cannot personally participate in that love, since he is not his parents' equal. Only as he watches them can he develop an understanding of marital love and bonding.

This kind of learning will influence him throughout life,

particularly when he chooses his own mate. Not only will his choice of a mate reflect what he saw in his parents' marriage, but the kind of marriage he builds will be based on the pattern they set, and on his unconscious assumption of what married love is and how two people ought to communicate. Does one person dictate to another, or do both participate in problem-solving? Are they selective in what they share, keeping the rest as secrets, or do they trust each other with who they are? Are they torn in their loyalties, allowing family or work or church to usurp each other's place in their lives, or do they value each other deeply, choosing each other over all conflicting demands?

If his parents have learned to love each other as equals, the child will instinctively pursue that kind of relationship in his own marriage. It will be deeply ingrained in him as the way marriage ought to be. But if they have resisted that kind of bonding with each other and instead have kept secrets or triangulated, bringing another person into the relationship or using the child as a go-between, he will learn that direct communication is either impossible or undesirable.

If *he* is the third party who is drawn in, as is often the case, the problem will be compounded. Not only is he not equipped to be either confidant or surrogate companion to a parent, but he will feel that he has to choose sides, gaining the approval of one parent at the expense of the other. Assuming an adult role before he has the maturity to handle it, he will develop a pseudomaturity. He will cover up his need to be dependent on a supportive adult, his need to know that someone older and wiser is in charge. He won't learn how to trust, but will decide that he has only himself to depend on, and will build his whole world around creating and taking advantage of triangles.

Naturally, parents cannot shut the child out of what goes on between them, determining to keep their relationship and their problems entirely to themselves. A child is tuned in to what goes on between Mom and Dad; they are the most important people in his life. Parents need to strike a balance, sharing at least what is necessary for the child to understand his own role and responsibility. If he picks up the feelings without the information needed to understand them, his immediate response will be to fantasize that *he* has somehow been responsible for the problem or that Mom and Dad might end up abandoning not only each other but him as well. A youngster needs to know that when there is a problem, his parents are going to do something about it and that the family relationships will survive.

• Sexuality. A growing child should learn from his parents what it means to be a sexual being. He needs to gain enough perception of his parents' sexuality to know that it is integral to their relationship.

Parents sometimes wonder when they should begin to teach their children about sex. Little do they realize that they *are* teaching them about sexuality from the time the children are infants. In their relating to each other, husband and wife communicate their sexual attitudes to their children, whether they are aware of it or not. The question is *what* they are communicating.

Children always know if there is a sexual relationship between their parents; it can't be disguised with a few hugs and pats. Time after time, in family sessions, I have asked a youngster, "How is it with Mom and Dad?" And invariably I get the right answer. How do they know? Because children are used to learning without words. We adults put everything into words, so that we can manage and process it. Children absorb the emotional content itself, without the distance of words.

Parents who have not worked out their sexual difficulties—who are seldom seen touching each other, who are tense in each other's presence, who deny their own sexuality—give their child a perception of what goes on in the bedroom. And they give him a message about what he ought to think of himself as a sexual being—the meaning of his own impulses and his own body and how his body is to be handled in other relationships.

When parents are uncomfortable with their sexuality or have not developed a caring, giving sexual relationship with each other, the message their child gets about marriage is one of sterility. The message he gets about himself is that there is something wrong with his sexuality, but he can't trust his parents to help him with it. If they can't deal with their own sexual difficulties, how can they be counted on to deal with his confusion and fears?

In such a situation, some children will learn to fear their impulses, look with suspicion on their bodies, and guiltily quell their questions about sex. More often, though, they will overvalue their own sexuality and, in the absence of input from their parents, drive their questions into fantasy. There the questions breed temptation and guilt in the conscience-ridden child, or erupt in impulsive behavior in a young person who doesn't have constraints.

Parents who are comfortable in their sexuality and are enjoying their sexual relationship with each other communicate that goodness to their children. They need not go out of their way to say sex is good; their children will know it intuitively. As they discover their own developing sexuality they will feel free to come to Mom or Dad with questions. They won't feel ashamed or guilty about their bodies and, although they may be confused about sex, they won't feel a need to resolve that confusion in furtive fantasy. When they are ready to enter marriage, one of the gifts carried over from their parents' marriage will be a healthy sense of their own sexuality and an understanding of how to use and enjoy it in their own marital bonding.

Beyond Behavior

Children see the world in very simple moral terms: If something is wrong, either I did it or someone else did it. And the usual conclusion is, "I did it." Young children, only a little removed from the assumed omnipotence of infancy, perceive themselves as the cause of whatever is going on in the family, including their parents' relationship. If a child picks up a sense that all is not well with Mom and Dad—if he senses sexual or emotional aridity, unhappiness or hostility between them—his world begins to feel very fragile. In his desire to relieve his anxiety, to be at peace, to keep his family and thus life together, he will subconsciously conjure up the notion, "If *I* had been different, things wouldn't be this way."

With such an assumption, he has two options. Either he can work hard to be very good, or he can create so many problems that somebody will have to sit up and take notice that he is hurting.

Although not every instance of misbehavior can be marked down to parental problems, many of the chronic behavior problems of childhood are not so much moral as emotional issues that can be traced back to a troubled marriage. When a child's needs are being met—the need to be loved consistently, the need for structure and control, the need for Mom and Dad to have a healthy and joyful marriage—he will listen to his parents. He will want to obey his parents because obeying brings closeness with them; it brings the sharing and openness that he so desperately needs.

But when he senses trouble, all he cares about is whether war is going to erupt in his family and split up his parents' marriage. That's the center that holds his world together. If he senses that center slipping or splitting, in spite of his efforts to obey, depression and fear will set in. Not knowing or believing that he can reach his parents, he will unconsciously act out his pain in misbehavior. He may steal or violate rules or break things or torment younger children or animals. He will be intractable, seemingly impervious to correction.

The family who sees that as just a discipline problem misses the point. The child is hurting and his hurt is reflecting the pain in the family. He is creating problems to solve problems, testing to see if there is anyone who can relieve his anxiety. Parents need to take notice and to seek the meaning behind their child's behavior. Then they need to deal with the disruptions in their own relationship. The temptation to blame family problems on a "bad" child can be strong. But if parents can muster the courage to face and resolve their own marital difficulties, they will discover that together they have the resources to give their children what they need, and their children will no longer need to misbehave to find security.

Surprisingly, perhaps, a chronically "perfect" child may be hiding as much pain as the misbehaver. Christian families are unique in that they usually place higher expectations on their children. When those expectations are not offset by the parents communicating warmth, support, and a genuine appreciation of their children, there is a great risk that the youngsters will develop an overwhelming sense of guilt or inadequacy or be plagued by other emotional difficulties.

I remember Kristin, the daughter of Christian parents who had a prominent place both in their community and in their church. More highly respected people could not be found anywhere, and their children were successful and well-behaved.

For Kristin, the second daughter, being a model child took a dangerous turn the summer of her sixteenth birthday, when she started dieting. Not content with dropping a few extra pounds, she became obsessed with achieving an ever more perfect body—which to her meant the ultimate in thinness. It was as if all the inner pressure she felt to be perfect, and all her longings for acceptance, were channeled into that one goal: to be as thin as she possibly could. She made it down to eighty-seven pounds and then collapsed.

Hospitalization saved her life, initially, but in the long run what really saved her was that her parents were eventually able to accept their role in her problem. It was naturally difficult for them to see, at first, how their lifestyle and expectations of themselves and their children had been translated by Kristin into a deadly attempt to achieve ultimate perfection.

Their love for Kristin and their other children, though shrouded by layers of expectations, was genuine. That was relatively easy to get to. What was more difficult was for them to get back to their feelings for each other, since these had likewise been buried in the demands of their lives. As it turned out, at the time Kristin started her dieting, their marriage had been at a crisis point from lack of emotional input. It was as if Kristin, at an unconscious level, had sensed the danger, had been frightened by the possibility of the marriage's collapse, and had acted out the emotionally starved relationship by starving herself.

In a sense, her unconscious tactic worked. In their alarm over their daughter's deteriorating condition, the husband and wife were drawn together with an intensity that had been missing for several years. As we worked through the issues that were uncovered and they rediscovered their love for each other, their concerns about appearance and achievement began to take second place to concerns about the emotional health of their family. In finding new peace and security with each other, they were able to let go of the anxiety that had driven them without their even being aware of it. Naturally, their children began to sense new freedom and security in their family.

Kristin's battle with anorexia was a tough one, and she had to work through some painful issues both individually and with her parents, but she made it. It was beautiful to see how her health and ability to receive both physical and emotional nurturance improved on a course parallel to that of her parents' marriage.

Who's Responsible Here?

When I work with non-Christian families, I frequently need to help them formulate values and develop structure in their homes. But when I work with Christians, I may have to help them focus not so much on standards of behavior and performance but on helping their children develop a realistic view of themselves. I often encounter an exaggerated sense of guilt in these children. They take their parents' admonitions seriously and literally and too often generalize these into a sense that all life revolves around doing right and avoiding wrong. Believing that their behavior has an almost magical impact on all the events in their world, they become so responsible that they are not able to distinguish what responsibility actually does lie with them and what lies with someone else. They can become paralyzed with the fear that they will do something wrong and bring disaster on themselves and their family.

Since a child's expectation of himself to always be right cannot be fulfilled, it sets him up for depression unless his parents temper their administration of right and wrong with warmth and support and an understanding of what can realistically be expected from children at different stages of growth. Above all, parents need to communicate that the welfare of the family, and their child's right to a valued place in that family, do *not* depend on his being perfect. They need to demonstrate and communicate that *they* and not the child are responsible for the family's security.

The Dilemma of Discipline
No matter how good a job parents are doing, sooner or later all children will misbehave. In responding to wrongdoing, Christian parents need to simultaneously communicate "I love you" and "You must obey." Just as in their marriage, love must persist even in the midst of working through conflicts and problems, so in their parenting the child needs the bedrock of the knowledge that he is loved even in the midst of discipline and limit setting. The love may not always feel warm and gooey, but that isn't what the child needs, anyway. What he needs is the unshakable conviction that his parents can feel with him and are acting

on his behalf, and that his needs are important.

Sometimes in their anxiety to do things right, parents can be so intense that they unwittingly communicate that love must be earned by perfect behavior. They will exert excessive controls and mete out strong punishments to ensure that their children are good. But children are no more capable than their parents are of always doing the right thing, and such a message is ultimately defeating. The Apostle Paul warned, "Fathers, do not provoke or irritate or fret, your children—do not be hard on them or harass them; lest they become discouraged and sullen and morose and feel inferior and frustrated; do not break their spirit" (Colossians 3:21, AMP). Intimidation and coercion may indeed succeed in producing controlled behavior—but at the expense of the children's individuality, creativity, and spontaneity. They will become automatons rather than the unique individuals God intended them to be.

The goal of discipline is *not* good behavior per se. Ideally, discipline is to teach not only about sin but also about the nature and value of the person. When disciplined in love, a child learns experientially what justice, mercy, and forgiveness are.

Parents all make mistakes and retrospect is a marvelous teacher. In the midst of stress and conflict and displeasure with a child's behavior, it is difficult to know whether coming on strong will encourage him to master himself or will discourage him. What's more, the course of action that may at one time encourage and support can at another defeat.

There are no formulas. You can't, from the behavior itself, infallibly prescribe the kind of discipline that will be the most constructive. The prescription must grow out of the parent-child relationship and be arrived at through an empathic understanding of the child and the situation. In order to discipline constructively, parents must be able to feel what their children are going through and to understand the meaning behind the behavior. Love and empathy should mingle with justice, in order for parents to give their children the training they need. And after all, isn't that how the Lord deals with us? As the psalmist wrote:

> *The Lord is compassionate and gracious,*
> *slow to anger, abounding in love.*
> *He will not always accuse,*
> *nor will He harbor His anger forever;*
> *He does not treat us as our sins deserve*
> *or repay us according to our iniquities.*
> *For as high as the heavens are above the earth,*
> *so great is His love for those who fear Him;*
> *as far as the east is from the west,*
> *so far has He removed our transgressions from us.*
> *As a father has compassion on his children,*
> *so the Lord has compassion*
> *on those who fear Him;*
> *for He knows how we are formed,*
> *He remembers that we are dust. . . .*
> *From everlasting to everlasting*
> *the Lord's love is with those who fear Him*
> *(Psalm 103:8-14, 17).*

To gauge discipline accurately, you must be able to bridle your own anger, or your perception of what is going on will be blurred. The parent who blindly strikes out in fury communicates lack of control; the world he portrays to his child is dangerous and unpredictable, with consequences that do not necessarily correspond to the child's actions. Yet at the same time, your anger cannot be so muted that there is no intensity behind what you say and do and stand for.

Obviously the potential for error is great. That is why both parents need to be involved in the process of discipline. Just as in solving other problems of daily life, they need to talk to each other, helping each other to understand their children and giving each other feedback on how they relate to them. "What do you think she was feeling?"

"What do you suppose made him do that?" "You were too hard on him." "You weren't strict enough."

If parents work together to understand and discipline their children, they can be both strong enough and flexible enough to give their children what they need. If they make a mistake—and mistakes are unavoidable—they can always admit their mistake and apologize. Children are very forgiving, because their need for their parents is so deep. In the process of discipline and mutual forgiveness, children learn more powerfully than through the most eloquent sermon on what law and grace are all about.

Sibling Rivalry

Kate put her hands to her throbbing temples and tried to block out the rising crescendo of her daughters' argument. They had been at it all day, and Kate was exhausted from trying to referee.

What parent has not cried in despair or anger or both, "*Why* can't you kids get along?" Christian parents especially may wonder where they went wrong in teaching brotherly (and sisterly) love.

But the fact is that some conflict and competition among siblings are normal. They are part of the growth process, part of learning to function socially and deal with conflict. In battling things out with brothers and sisters, children determine what their roles and territory are and define their relationships with their parents and with each other. In itself, sibling rivalry, though it may be tiresome and exasperating to a parent, is not a sign that something has gone seriously wrong.

This rivalry presents both a pitfall and an opportunity. Parents can inadvertently exacerbate the rivalry if they allow themselves to identify with one child over the others and thus make it necessary for the others to fight all the harder for the attention and significance they crave.

There are many reasons a parent may develop special feelings for a certain child. Perhaps that child was particularly desired, as is often the case with the firstborn. Perhaps the child was born at a time when Father was traveling a lot and Mother was feeling tense and lonely. Perhaps the family was under particular financial pressure or, perhaps was feeling comfortable and secure after years of striving for a particular standard of living.

Whatever the reason, it sometimes happens that parents will feel an especially strong inner bond with one child and inadvertently create a triangle. If that happens, the other children must find some way to break through, and their war with the brother or sister ensues.

The middle child has sometimes been identified as the one who feels the strongest need to work hard to get parental attention. One can make too much of that assumption—there are so many factors besides position in the family that influence a child's personality and behavior—but it can indeed happen that the middle child is more prone to be left out. The oldest child, being first, may be the most prized or, being the one with whom they were learning how to be parents, the one about whom parents feel the most guilt. The youngest may have received the most attention simply because he or she was the youngest and seemed always to need more help than the other children. But what claims does the middle child have?

Parents need to examine their attitudes and see if they are unintentionally setting up a situation that encourages rather than diffuses sibling rivalry. Are they meeting the needs of *all* their children? Are they valuing each of their children as individuals, in spite of any special emotional bond they may feel with one of them? Are they avoiding scapegoating one child, singling him or her out as the source of all problems without stopping to examine what that child's behavior might mean? Are they working out marital difficulties between themselves, refraining from confiding in or depending on one of their children?

The opportunity offered by sibling rivalry is that it becomes a safe arena in which children can learn, with the help of their parents, how to relate to others in healthy and constructive ways. In the protected environment of the family they may both learn and fail without detriment to themselves. Out in the world they will be thrown into relationships in which people don't trust or care for each other, where the competition may be fierce and where they may not be valued. The family bonds afford a secure place for learning how to compete and yet maintain their own integrity in the confidence of an enduring relationship.

Does this mean that parents should patiently tolerate their children's fighting, so as not to interfere with the growth process? By no means. For one thing, parents have a legitimate need for peace and order in their household, and they have a right to ask for it. For another thing, they owe it to their children to step in and set limits. The children don't know how to do it for themselves; a parent must take charge or the children will feel out of control. Parents must teach as well as model how relationships and their inevitable conflicts can be managed.

Letting Go, Letting Grow
Having children is a risk. By the very nature of things, parenthood is a job given to people who have had no previous experience. The child that comes to them is an unknown quantity; parents cannot predict or prescribe who he will be or how he will turn out. And they don't know what successes or failures will result from their parenting.

My wife and I did not do a perfect job raising our children. No parents have. If the requirement were that parents produce perfect children, the prospects of parenthood would be frightening indeed. But perfection is not the goal. The most important requirement is that children remain secure in the knowledge of their relationship with their parents, yet not be bound to them in dependency. The goal is to produce children who can think and feel and can be freely, completely, uniquely themselves. A child who knows he has the freedom to tell his parents what is going on inside of him will develop the kind of healthy dependency and security that will prepare him for independence as he grows.

How do parents give that to a child? By giving it first of all to each other. The husband and wife who have learned to know and accept each other as unique individuals and have let each other inside in an unseverable bond will naturally bestow on their children the same kind of bonding and freedom. Respect and caring will be givens that underlie all their interactions with their children.

At every phase of a child's development, the question recurs: Is my objective that my child belong to himself? Can I take the risk that he might fail and that, by implication, I too will fail? Can I risk losing him? The first time a child crosses a street on his own is a moment of high anxiety for the parent. The urge to hold on is strong. Trusting the child's increasing ability to take care of himself means you have to trust yourself. You have to know that you have given the child what he needs, and that he will not need to search for his security by acting out.

It is a delicate balance that parents need to achieve. If they hold too tightly out of uncertainty about themselves or their marriage, they prevent the child from learning that it is okay for him to be himself. Thus he will either cling in dependency or strike out in pseudoindependence, never developing an inner core of confidence.

If parents hold their child too loosely, not becoming involved enough in his life or providing the structure and control he needs at critical stages of his life, he will feel adrift, unsure of who he is or where he belongs. Parents are usually well aware of the need to provide controls and structure for the young child, but it is during adolescence that a child is most in need of controls and structure. It is then that his identity is in flux and his efforts at self-discovery can take dangerous turns through drugs, sex, or deviant behavior. If a firm relationship is lacking at home, he will take his need for belonging elsewhere. That is why teenagers are so quick to adopt and cling to the values of their peer culture. They are looking for a family, a place to belong, a structure that will give them identity.

The Legacy We Leave

Unfortunately, the sins of the fathers do affect the third and fourth generation. Whatever has not been resolved between the parents will have an effect on the child. If the problems in marriage are not worked out, the child will inherit the need to resolve them inside himself. I see this over and over again in family generational patterns.

Yet it is by no means a hopeless, irreversible process. God has built into each marriage the potential for change, for seeing and doing things differently. As husband and wife, with the Lord's help, redeem the mistakes from their own past through their interaction and bonding with each other, they create a climate in which their children are not bound by the failings of past generations but are free to grow as healthy individuals. As the children strike out on their own, they will carry not the burdens of generations of family problems but the freedom their parents have won by tackling those problems together and arriving at a new way of being.

When parents have successfully separated from their own families and solidified a new, unique bond with each other, their children reap the benefits of that bond in their own successful bonding to and separating from the parents. As they enter a bonding relationship with their own spouses, the process comes full circle in a continuing, upward spiral.

t w e l v e

Preserving the Future

We've come full circle. A man and woman fall in love and marry, creating a bond that harks back to their origins and will later set the stage for their children's marriages. It is a cycle that continues on, generation after generation—each new family unique and yet reflective of all who have gone before and prophetic of all who are to come.

But the progress of the family is not necessarily steady. In fact, in recent years, families in western society have been floundering as never before, as marriages sicken and die in ever increasing numbers. During the 1970s, nearly half of all marriages broke up. By the mid-1980s, United States Census Bureau statistics showed that more than a quarter of families with children under age eighteen were headed by a single parent. If predictions hold, the 1990s will see between one-third and one-half of American families with only a single parent.

The church has not been immune. Families have been crumbling within our walls at a pace that lags not far behind the outside world.

The effects of this deterioration were reflected in a recent Gallup survey. Among college students who identified themselves as evangelical, only slightly more than half of the respondents said they believed premarital sex was wrong, and twenty-eight percent had sex regularly or occasionally; thirty percent had had more than one sexual partner.

I don't believe the prevalence of premarital sexual activity, even among Christian young people, can be blamed solely on the sexually permissive society in which we live. Sexuality is a natural drive in the adolescent and young-adult years, but one that can be contained within appropriate boundaries when all else is going well. But when the parents of these young people are themselves betraying or leaving their marriages, they send a message to their children that there is no point in preserving the sanctity of marriage.

My clinical impression is that the youngsters who are the most driven to be sexually active are those for whom something was missing in those early years of bonding. Carrying within themselves an ongoing, unmet need for connectedness, and seeing little outside themselves to prohibit sexual activity, they are tempted to feed their inner hunger however they can.

Christian marriages are under continuous attack, and our young people are floundering, at risk themselves for ending up in precarious or unhealthy relationships. What are we doing about it? We must do something! The church cannot afford to lose the families that are its very soul.

The church and the family, God's two great institutions, need each other for survival. They are the vehicles through which God has chosen to meet our deepest human needs, and their health determines our own.

Back to Basics
We must remember who we are. In the rush of daily living and in our scramble for wealth, position, and sensation, it's easy to forget God's original pronouncement: "It is not

good for the man to be alone" (Genesis 2:18). Whether or not we recognize it, we are people in need of relationship. Often we don't recognize it and can feel that we are driven by other needs. As youths we are driven by our sexuality. As middle-aged adults we are driven to succeed, get ahead, build our empire. When we reach old age, we are driven by the fear of loneliness.

But these drives of youth, middle age, and old age are really only expressions of a greater need and drive. It is not sexuality, power, or death; it is the need to be connected intimately to another human being, and not to be alone, that persists throughout life.

The teenager's drive for sex is fueled by a terror of alienation, of being alone. In illicit sex, young people believe they can manufacture the kind of closeness they yearn for.

As young people grow into adulthood they begin to search for satisfaction in careers, but neither the executive's skill nor the tradesman's tool nor the artist's craft fills the need. Why has the cocktail party become an adjunct to many businesses? Is it not that the cocktails seem to help one feel more at ease in relating to others?

Our need for relationship begins the moment we draw our first breath and lingers until we draw our last. Indeed, it will be with us throughout eternity. From the moment we first open our eyes we are looking for that link with another person. What some have called the life force is not the drive to succeed but the more basic drive to be secure.

And what is the deepest level of security that we yearn for? The security of utter acceptance and absolute love in an enduring relationship.

The acute pain and fear of aloneness are part of the drive for marriage that even pushes people beyond living together. The need for intimacy is satisfied only by the assurance of permanence. Some may think marriage as an institution is out of fashion, but the longing is very contemporary; as long as it persists, so will the need and desire for marriage.

The Church's Mission to Marriages

If the church is to carry on its mission to bring the good news of redemption to a hurting world, it must awake to the pain of the individuals and families in its midst. It must clearly affirm the goodness of God's provision for marriage.

For years we have focused our vision and our efforts on the mission field "out there," and rightly so. Can we, without losing that vision, heighten our awareness of the urgent needs in our own congregations? Marriages today are having to withstand fierce attack, and many are wounded or dying. I believe it is urgent that the church ask itself some pointed questions about its role in caring for its own people.

In Christ we have the resources necessary to combat all that would destroy us. Paul wrote:

> *Be strong in the Lord and in His mighty power. Put on the full armor of God so that you can take your stand against the devil's schemes. For our struggle is not against flesh and blood, but against the rulers, against the authorities, against the powers of this dark world and against the spiritual forces of evil in the heavenly realms. Therefore put on the full armor of God, so that when the day of evil comes, you may be able to stand your ground, and after you have done everything, to stand"* (Ephesians 6:10-13).

If we believe that we have the resources to combat the disintegration of marriage, we need to look at steps we can take to apply that power effectively.

I believe that the church can minister to marriages through its *leadership*, through its *program*, and through *referral* to competent helpers for those who are hurting. Of these resources, the most powerful is the church leadership, since it sets the tone for the ministries of the other two.

Leading Others to Wholeness

The leadership of the church can play a powerful role in providing the kind of help marriages need today. Not only what is said from the pulpit but the character of the leaders themselves has tremendous impact on what happens in the church as a whole.

• The power of the pulpit. There are limits to what can be accomplished merely through speaking to people, but the pulpit can indeed be a powerful force in ministering to marriages and families. Those who speak to the church can encourage openness (both by exhortation and example) among the people, minister to the fear of intimacy, and endorse marriage as a good and satisfying provision of God despite the problems that exist. They can warn God's people of the dangers of carelessly adopting society's attitudes toward marriage and its willingness to abandon family life in favor of finding fulfillment elsewhere. They can alert their listeners to the reality of the struggles many families in their midst are facing, and can encourage acceptance and constructive help rather than condemnation for those who are floundering. They can voice their commitment to take marriage and the family seriously and to support church programs that foster family life and allow for its expression within the church.

• The effectiveness of example. "Every man feels instinctively that all the beautiful sentiments in the world weigh less than a single lovely action." So wrote American poet and essayist James Russell Lowell; and though his words were written more than a hundred years ago, they express an enduring truth. Actions *do* speak more loudly than words. In the 1980s the church learned that truth in a painful way as one after another of its visible spokesmen succumbed to immorality. No matter what is said from the pulpit, it is what is demonstrated by the lives and characters of those in leadership that will send a lasting message.

When the Apostle Paul compiled his lists of qualifications necessary for those who would lead the church, he did not prescribe eloquence. Instead he focused on the qualities of character and patterns of life required of overseers and deacons (1 Timothy 3:1-13; Titus 1:6-9).

It is notable that in both lists, the family life of the potential leader occupies a significant place. Those who lead the church are to be successful in their family relationships first (1 Timothy 3:2, 4-5, 12; Titus 1:6). Although Paul did not take the time in these particular passages to describe in detail what family life should be like, his convictions are clear in other writings (see especially Ephesians 5:21-6:4). The leader's family is to be a living, vibrant demonstration of the love, respect, and intimacy that God desires for marriages and families.

Unfortunately, many church leaders today satisfy these family requirements more in form than in substance. Yes, they have remained the husband of one wife, and their children, for the most part, have kept out of serious trouble. But what are their family relationships really like? Are they committed to their wives, giving them first place above all rivals, including their work? Do they cultivate intimacy and sharing in their marriages, listening to their wives' needs and disclosing their own, letting their partners into deepest recesses of their souls, honoring their mates as equal participants in the struggles and decisions of life?

We are all prone to hide ourselves for the sake of a good impression; we all are tempted to pursue fulfillment in activity rather than relationship. I suspect that those who lead the church may encounter even tougher battles in these areas.

Bob was the popular pastor of a large metropolitan church. His Sunday morning sermons were broadcast over the local radio station and he figured prominently in the civic life of his city. His calendar of speaking engagements was usually filled a year in advance, and he served on the board of two Christian organizations. His life had a tremendous impact.

Especially on his family. His wife, left on her own a good

part of every week, leaned heavily on her teenage sons for emotional support and help around the house. It never occurred to her that she had a right to her husband's time and attention, let alone intimacy with such an important servant in God's kingdom.

Bob's sons felt vaguely frustrated and distant from their father. But having been brought up to make a good impression for the sake of the church, they drove their feelings underground. And besides, how could they be angry with a dad who was doing such a good job of God's work?

Bob truly did have a great impact on the church and community, but very little of this supported family life or demonstrated the importance of marriage. No one who saw him would guess that he was a person with needs and weaknesses, someone who needed the closeness and strength of an intimate marriage. He didn't know it himself. Up on his pedestal, he didn't realize that it was not good for him to be alone. In all his giving to church and community, he protected himself from giving himself, at the deepest level, to his wife. His successes shielded him from his loneliness; when he felt it at all, it was a nameless gnawing that was easily stilled by throwing himself even more fervently into his work.

Bob would not verbally deny the importance of marriage and family. Indeed, his church was very strict in its opposition to divorce. But no one observing his life would catch a glimmer of the true importance of marriage. No one watching him would be reminded that marriage is God's solution to man's deepest needs. The message that filtered into Bob's congregation from his example was that it was important to be active and successful in the work of the church, to create a flawless impression, and to appear to be above daily human needs.

Bob himself was not entirely to blame for this situation. Everyone and everything around him encouraged him to continue along this route. His wife rarely complained or made demands on their marriage. The church enjoyed having a celebrity as a pastor and wanted to believe that it was indeed possible to be self-sufficient and successful in the Christian life. The whole Christian world around him subtly whispered, "Give yourself to God's work. Be busy. Don't pay attention to your limitations. Do more and more, and God will repay you by providing for your family. Don't give in to weak, fleshly, lazy longings to spend time enjoying your wife and children. Be hard on yourself. Trust the Lord and go it alone."

Christian leaders need to wake up to the necessity of demonstrating the importance of family closeness. Their words can keep congregations conforming to the outward forms of physically intact families, but it is only their lives that will impress others with the necessity and rewards of having one's life intertwined with another's in living, loving union.

Programming for Family Life

When the leadership of the church is committed, both in word and example, to strengthening family life, it can start a process that reaches into the structure and programs of the church and touches individual families at their point of need. It is not enough to adopt a passive, hands-off approach to family life within the church. Churches, by their structure and programs *do* affect family life. The question is whether the effect is positive or negative.

Look at any church calendar or bulletin of coming events. How many church activities and programs are geared to support marriages and families? How many actively contribute to the enhancement of marriage and family life? How many provide help for marriages and families in trouble?

When the structure and programs of a church are not designed to support family life, chances are they are detracting from it. In some churches it is possible for families never to have all their members in the same place at the same time as they attend various church functions. Some churches have so much going on that people are drained dry through the work of the church and have little left to give their families. While this itself will not necessarily split up a family, it does send a message about the importance of the family.

Churches need to be purposeful in planning programs that support family life. They can form classes and training groups that foster communication between the generations, give guidance in parenting, or speak to specific issues that affect families. They can recognize the reality that some marriages and families are hurting, and they can provide support groups for those families that are already in difficulty.

Some churches are able to provide counseling by a church staff member or counseling center. This is not possible for all churches, though; often, when a church is large enough to support such a service, it is also likely to have more problems than one staff person or counseling service can handle.

What the church needs is not necessarily individual specialists but an overall structure that says, "Marriages and families are more important than activities, programs, or even Christian service. Scripture gives marriage a prominent place in God's plan for our growth and welfare and for the advancement of His kingdom—and so will we. Not only will we guard against structures and programs that erect barriers between family members or pull them away from each other, but we will actively seek to provide what marriages and families need to grow in love and unity. And we will work to make this church a safe, uncondemning place for those who are hurting, so that they may be helped rather than driven away."

No one church can do everything or guarantee the safety and welfare of its families. But most can do more than they are. And it's worth it. The church needs the strength of thriving families and the vitality of the love generated when families are enjoying the life the Lord intended for them.

Pointing the Way to Help

No church, no matter how well-grounded the leadership or the programs, can provide for every need or marital difficulty. Sometimes the best service the church can offer is to direct its people to outside help, particularly when the problems are serious or long-standing.

Working with marriages and families is in some ways a specialty, so it is important to direct hurting couples to someone who will be well-qualified to help. It is not necessary for a counselor or therapist to have a string of degrees after his or her name to be effective, but it is important that he or she have training in marital or family therapy.

Churches would do well to become part of a network, getting to know agencies and counselors in their area to whom they can refer their people. It is not hard to develop such connections. Local pastors, physicians, and sometimes even attorneys, will often have a list of practitioners to whom they have found they can confidently refer couples. In addition, licensing and accrediting organizations, such as the American Association for Marriage and Family Therapy, are good sources of referral information.

If the church has created a climate in which its people feel free to seek help when they need it, and if it can direct them to competent helpers, it will have done well as a channel of God's grace to His people.

A Legacy for Eternity

In this world, marriage will always be imperfect, incomplete. But if what Scripture says about marriage is true, it need never be stale. It can be greatly satisfying, a gift of grace not only to the couples themselves but to their families, their churches, and to a hurting world around them. The church owes it not only to itself and its people but to the Lord to work for the welfare of marriage. When the church can foster marriages that truly reflect her own relationship with the Lord, her potential for benefit to the world will be boundless, measurable only by eternity.

endnotes

1. A.W. Tozer, *The Knowledge of the Holy* (New York: Harper & Row, 1961), 107.

2. C.S. Lewis, *The Four Loves* (New York: Harcourt, Brace Jovanovich, 1960), 54.

3. The Hebrew word for *flesh* or *body* was often paralleled by the word for *soul*, referring to the totality of one's being.

4. C.S. Lewis, *The Four Loves*, 183–184.

5. Phyllis Theroux, "Mother Hate," *Parents*, August 1989, 46–49.

6. Quoted in *Christianity Today*, 14 July 1989, 39.

7. R.V.G. Tasker, *The Gospel According to St. Matthew* (Grand Rapids: Eerdmans, 1961).